Microsoft Dynamics CRM

Compiled by Terry Sanchez-Clark

Microsoft Dynamics CRM

ISBN: 978-1-60332-031-3

Edited By: Jamie Sever

Table of Contents

Introduction

Microsoft Dynamics CRM is a Customer Relationship Management software package developed by Microsoft. It is a part of the Microsoft Dynamics family of business tools.

The current version of Dynamics is 3.0, released on December, 2005. The most notable update over the version 1.2 (version 2 was skipped entirely), is the ability to synchronize with Microsoft Outlook, and integration with BlackBerry mobile devices.
The mindset for acquiring customer relationship management (CRM) solutions is no longer about simply adding technology but rather about buying solutions that fit into your existing business environment and that your people will actually use.

This 31-page guide takes you through evaluating Microsoft Dynamics CRM version 3.0, giving you a fuller understanding of how it is designed to work the way you do, work the way your business does, and work the way technology should.

Essential areas of information addressed include the following:

* How Microsoft CRM meets your business needs both today and in the future by providing you with powerful features, flexible deployment options, and transparent migration;

* Features and capabilities that address core CRM activities such as demand creation, marketing, customer service, and mobile CRM;

* User-based design that offers an improved interface, seamless integration with key software programs such as Microsoft Office, and increased access to CRM data for use well beyond the traditional sales-related context;

* An extensive list of resources that add value to the Microsoft CRM solutions;

Issues on Functions Affecting: Entities, Fields, Accounts, Attributes

Question 1: Deactivate entities

There are some entities that the office will be using in this system, such as Accounts, Invoices, Competitors and so on.

What can I do to deactivate these entities without deleting them to make the menus simple and easy for users?

A: You can control it with the help of 'roles'. If you don't want a user to see invoices than remove that user's access to invoices from his role.

Question 2: Export Attributes List to Excel

In MS CRM, in the window where you see columns and rows, there is an option available to "Export to Excel". I want to document my system by producing spreadsheets of each entity, listing the "Stock" attributes and properties as well as the "New" attributes and properties. When in the Attributes window of any given entity there seems to be no option to "Export to Excel".

What can I do to document my system?

A: The stock attributes are available in the downloadable planning documents from Microsoft. This, at least, saves you from printing those. There is no Excel option, but you could export customizations to an XML file from the Setup menu.

Question 3: Select more than 1 object in the lookup field

I would like to have the ability to select more than one object in a lookup field. Is there a way to accomplish this?

A: No. The only exception to this is the party list like the 'to', 'cc' and 'bcc' fields in an email, but this is an internal thing and cannot be used in customizations.

Question 4: Changes in Account owner ID

Why do changes in Account Owner ID affect the Incident Owner ID?

A: This is due to the Reassign Cascade Setting, whenever the parent (Account) gets reassigned (change of owner), the child object (Case) also gets reassigned.

To change this setting in Microsoft CRM v3.0:

Microsoft CRM Web Client >> Settings >> Customizations >> select the Account entity >> Relationship >> find the Account (Primary Entity) to Case (Related Entity) Type of Behavior: "Parental" entry;

Open this relationship entry and change the type of behavior from "Parental to "Configurable Cascading" then update the "Assign" value from "Cascade All" to your choice. "Cascade none" is a good default choice.

Question 5: User specific customization

For example: User A would like to go to the accounts section and have "my active accounts" as his default view. User B wants a custom view we have created called "active accounts ending contract" to be the default. The system administrators and managers want the default view for them to be "Active Accounts".

Within these default views certain columns are wanted by User A that User B does not want.

User A wants address to show as a column but User B does not want the address shown.

Is there a way for each user to customize their default views and columns shown in the views?

Is this possible and if so how can we accomplish this?

A: There is only one default view for each entity in a CRM installation. All users will have the same default view. If different users want different versions of the same view, then they must create new views customized to their needs.

Question 6: Update field in Entity A when Entity B is saved in CRM

I have created two custom entities and I would like to be able to do the following:

When a date is added to a field on Entity B and Entity B is then saved, I want to update a date field on Entity A (with the date that was entered on Entity B plus a year).

How can I do this?

A: One way of doing this is by using callouts. You can write an 'Update' callout for Entity. Within this you can create the object of Entity A and update it as required.

Question 7: Managing Customizations

I have not found much written on approaches to managing customizations, i.e. keeping track of what we've changed, having an approach to rolling back changes, having an orderly approach to managing changes into production, etc. Even as simple as it is to tailor the CRM application, I would hope that people are not just making changes on the fly in their production CRM system.

Are companies exporting/archiving the XML export files to 'SourceSafe' as a means to managing versions?

What approach is good to keep changes organized and tracked?

A: The OrgUIBase is a great resource. In addition, my old organization used to keep extensive details for each customization iteration, which included (but is not limited to) the following:

1. Excel PivotTable based off of the data in FilteredOrganizationUI view.
2. Excel based UI Mock-up of each "release" (though the folks at Invoke have a very handy Visio based CRM 3.0 UI Template.
3. Excel Based Log of all customized data fields.
4. Folders for each "Release" with subfolders for all entities + date of release.
5. All .xml customization exports (for each individual entities been updated, as well as all entities in a given release).
6. All JavaScript code, per Data Field and Form in a given entity and dependencies.
7. All updates to the web.config, isv.config.xml, and the Sitemap.
8. CRM distribution list e-mails the day before a Publish and the day after with applicable User documentation, etc.
9. Folder for all ISV, Custom reports and various updates therein.
10. Folder for all Hot fixes, CRM Updates, etc.

Finally, we had a Test/Dev Server to build each release, then, we'd export each customization and Import to our Prod server. We never really deleted customizations, as were just getting into

3.0 before I left. Since I left this company in '05, I have been an MSCRM consultant. Not everyone goes to such lengths as my previous organization. Probably because many are smaller companies that just don't have a dedicated CRM Admin or, they just don't find the value in such extensive documentation, I suppose. But as a Consultant, we certainly document our initial customizations in much the same manner, and it is extremely valuable during User Acceptance Testing, and support issues, as we have dates, documentation, etc. should we have to rollback or remove fields, customizations, JavaScript, etc.

Question 8: Display labels as bold in a form

Is there any code that can be written so that a form's "onload" event would set an attribute's label to "bold?"

Is it possible to change the colors of labels to improve the readability of the form and help the user to hone in on specific portions of the form?

A: It's a web application so you can do almost everything you like. However, CRM uses the field required level to highlight required and recommended fields in the way you describe.

Question 9: Mapping fields

When I promote a lead to an opportunity, I want to have the same fields mapped. For example, Lead.Name - Opportunity.Name, etc. The opportunity to get the same information stored in the lead. I want to make the same thing for the contacts.

How is that possible?

A: You need to look into Mapping in CRM for this purpose.

1. Click Settings -> Customization ->;
2. Double click on 'Lead' to customize it.
3. New window will popup.
4. On the left navigation bar, click Relationships and then select type "Mappable".
5. Double click on the mapping you want to modify or create new mapping as per your requirement.

Question 10: Adding two days to a new datetime field

I have added a new date time field to my Entity: Lead called 'Contact By' (schema name new_contactbydate) that I would like to default to two days past the 'record create' date. I believe I need to do an OnSave event, but I don't really know quite what to put in there. Is there a good way to do this?

A: The example below gives you the basic idea:

The JScript should be placed in the Lead's OnLoad event. The code checks to see if it's a new 'Lead' or an 'updated Lead'. If it's a new lead, it retrieves the current date, adds 2 days, and put the result in your new Date/Time field.

```
var CRM_FORM_TYPE_CREATE = 1;
var CRM_FORM_TYPE_UPDATE = 2;
Var MyDate = new Date()
Var ContactBy = new Date (MyDate.getYear(),
MyDate.getMonth(), MyDate.getDate()+2)

switch (crmForm.FormType)
{
case CRM_FORM_TYPE_CREATE:
crmForm.all.new_contactbydate.DataValue = ContactBy
break;
case CRM_FORM_TYPE_UPDATE:
break;
}
```

Keep in mind that this will only work when leads are created. If the leads are imported, say from a Duns or a Convention list, you may want to make sure that you add a 'Contact By' column to your .csv or .txt file that has the appropriate date for "Contact By" in every import row.

You can check out Michael Höhne's website which is an excellent resource for real world JScript solutions at http://www.stunnware.com/crm2/topic.aspx?id=JS3. This website will tell you how to account for 'Leads' being created on the weekend, so that the 'Contact By' date is adjusted to the second business day.

Question 11: Adding Field Values

I would like added values in fields to give a total field value. There are 20 fields. Fields 1 to 19 have a value of, say 5 each. Field number 20 requires the total of 19 x 5.

How can I do this?

A: You can use JavaScript on Form onLoad or onSave to do it.

Sample code:

```
var sum = crmForm.all.[fieldname1].DataValue +
crmForm.all.[fieldname2].DataValue +
crmForm.all.[fieldname3].DataValue + ...

var total = sum * 5;

crmForm.all.[fieldname20].DataValue = total;
```

An alternative solution is to place the following code in "OnChange" event of your fields [1-19]:

```
crmForm.all.field20.DataValue=crmForm.all.field1.Data
Value+crmForm.all.field2.DataValue+crmForm.all.field3
.DataValue+.................+crmForm.all.field19.Data
Value;
```

You need to place this code in onchange event of every field [1-19] so that if you change value in any one of the fields, the changes will be reflected in field20 [Total].

You can use "fireonchange" method to avoid writing the code again and again.

Question 12: Multi-field search

I like to do an advanced search for all contacts belonging to any account from a particular industry sector. I can easily generate a list of all accounts that are marked as 'Durable Manufacturing' in the Industry field.

CRM 3.0 also allows us to generate a list of all 'Primary Contacts' from any accounts that have 'Durable Manufacturing' in the Industry field.

How can we generate a list of every contact from the 'Durable Manufacturing' industry?

A: You can do this by going to the 'advanced find' function and follow the next steps:

- Select Contact as "Look for".
- Select "Parent Customer (Account)". This is located under the relating attributes.
- Select industry and set this to 'Durable Manufacturing'.

Question 13: Defining access right issue

I have this security policy to implement:

I added a custom field sector to the account activity and I would manage access based on the value of this field. For example:

If the sector = "a", only users who have role "A" have the right to access and view the accounts that have the sector value ="a".

If the sector = "b", only users who have role "B" have the right to access and view the accounts that have the sector value ="b".

So can I define this access policy based on a custom field value?

A: No. This is not possible using this mechanism. However, if you create 2 child business units off the root business unit, you could assign the entire Role "A" people to one of the child units and all of the Role "B" people to the other child unit. Then, when a user with Role "A" creates a new account, the rest of the Role "A" people can view this record but not the Role "B" people and vice versa. This assumes that these users do not have 'Organization level' permissions, but instead have only Parent - Child Business Unit or less access.

Question 14: How to eliminate duplicate/obsolete usernames

How do you eliminate usernames that are entered in error or are no longer needed?

Setting up a new CRM installation, the domain had .lcl as part of the domain name. Entered the users without .lcl and it somehow authenticated when entering the user into CRM, yet it would not function properly for the user. Had to inactivate the original user, add the new user, and then everything seems to work ok.

Also, in such a case, I have problems with the duplicate username.

How can this be fixed? Or do we have to live with it?

A: There are no supported fixes here for you, but there are some unsupported ones.

You can manually delete the records from SystemUserBase, but there are several dependant tables you will also need to remove corresponding records from. The RI on the DB will tell you which ones as you try to delete the records.

If you have added the user with the .lcl suffix, you can always manually update the SystemUser table and change the column that stores this value. I believe it's the login col. I have done this w/o problem several times where the domain was left off when the user was added. This only works though if you have not already tried to add the user in with the correct login name.

Question 15: Received status code field phone call in callout is incorrect

I have some problems with the status code and state code fields of a phone call in a callout. When I close (option cancelled) a phone call, I get the status 1 ("open") in the field's status code and state code while I expect the status 3 ("cancelled"). The other fields of the activity are coming in correctly.

When retrieving the activity from the web service, I get the expected status 3 ("cancelled").

I'm using a PostUpdate callout and using the postImageEntityXml to find my properties.

Are there issues with this field?

A: You can try a PostSetState or PreSetState callout. This is the appropriate event to watch for status changes.

Question 16: Filtering activity types

I'm only interested in the sales module. I edited the "Salesperson" security role, and in the Service, Service Management and Marketing all the "dots" are empty, none selected. Let's say I applied the salesperson role to John. John logs into CRM and he clicks on 'Activities' under 'My work'. He can look for some activities selecting the date, 'Type' and a 'View'. Here is the interesting part for me. I want to make some changes at the 'Activity Type' so John can't see 'Service Activity', 'Campaign Activity' and 'Campaign Response Activity'.

Is this possible in any way?

A: No. You cannot filter the activity types for roles. You may create new views but you cannot restrict some activity types from users.

Question 17: Stuck with linked entity query

I'm a little stuck with building a query between a contact and a custom entity bank account. I want to retrieve all contacts with a specific bank account number should always return one (1) contact account. The query results in a soap error saying "Server was unable to process request".

I pasted the code below:

```
public contact GetContactByAccountNumber(string
accountnumber)
{
QueryExpression query = new QueryExpression();

query.EntityName = "contact";

ColumnSet columns = new ColumnSet();
columns.Attributes = new string[] { "firstname" };
query.ColumnSet = columns;

LinkEntity linkEntity1 = new LinkEntity();
linkEntity1.JoinOperator = JoinOperator.Natural;
linkEntity1.LinkFromEntityName = "contact";
linkEntity1.LinkFromAttributeName =
"new_bankaccountnumber";
linkEntity1.LinkToEntityName = "new_bankaccount";
linkEntity1.LinkToAttributeName =
"new_bankaccountnumber";

linkEntity1.LinkCriteria = new FilterExpression();
linkEntity1.LinkCriteria.FilterOperator =
LogicalOperator.And;

ConditionExpression condition1 = new
ConditionExpression();
condition1.AttributeName = "accountnumber";
condition1.Operator = ConditionOperator.Equal;
condition1.Values = new object[] { accountnumber };

linkEntity1.LinkCriteria.Conditions = new
ConditionExpression[] {
condition1 };

query.LinkEntities = new LinkEntity[] { linkEntity1
};
RetrieveMultipleRequest requests = new
RetrieveMultipleRequest();
requests.ReturnDynamicEntities = true;
requests.Query = query;
```

```
//retrieve the tasks
RetrieveMultipleResponse response =
(RetrieveMultipleResponse)_service.Execute(requests);
}
```

What can I do to correct this?

A: Your query in SQL format will be:

```
SELECT c.firstname FROM contact AS c
JOIN new_bankaccount AS b ON c.new_bankaccountnumber
=
b.new_bankaccountnumber
WHERE b.accountnumber = @accountnumber

Try replacing "b.accountnumber" with
"new_bankaccountnumber".
```

Question 18: Changing the modifiedon field in activities

Is it possible to change the modifiedon field to a different value in a postcallout?

A: Yes, but in an unsupported way. The only way to modify the createdon, createdby, modifiedon and modifiedby fields is through a direct SQL update call. If your aim for this is some kind of synchronization from another system where you would like to see the last modification date of the other system in the CRM record as well, you should consider adding a custom attribute to the entity and using it to store the date.

Question 19: Inheritance in CRM Developer

I need to implement a kind of inheritance, like the 'Activity' and its subtypes.

Is it possible?

A: No, it is not possible to have 'Activities' like relationship for your custom entity. This is the limitation of custom entities that you cannot have inheritance along with some other limitations. But there is always more than one way to solve a problem.

Question 20: Disable fields programmatically

How do I disable fields programmatically, and how to change the values to choose from a picklist when different values are selected from a radio button field?

A: You can do this:

```
// set it as readonly
crmForm.all.xxxfield.readOnly = true;
// OR set it as disabled
crmForm.all.xxxfield.disabled = true;
or
crmForm.all.xxxfield.setAttribute("disabled", true);
```

Question 21: Displaying duration between two dates

I have two 'Date Fields', Date1 and Date2. I want to display the duration from Date1 to Date2 in a text box.

How do I do this in Java Script?

A: You can use this code to get duration between two dates:

```
var date1 =crmForm.all.<date1fieldname>.DataValue;
var date2 =crmForm.all.<date2fieldname>.DataValue;
crmForm.all.<durationfieldname> .value=(date2-
date1)/( 60 * 60 * 1000);
```

Question 22: Disabling time field alone

How can I disable time field alone from date and time?

A: You can enable or disable the time selection box of a
date/time field using the following syntax:

```
var dateField = crmForm.all.<name of datetime field>;

//Check the existence of the time field. It is null
if the control is setup
to only display the date.
if (dateField.all.time != null) {

//Disable the time field
dateField.all.time.disable();

//Enable the time field
dateField.all.time.enable();
}
```

Question 23: Update a field with an automated value

I have a field, Case Title, I want to update with an automated value. The code is executed at the onSave event to create the value in the Case Title. In order that end users cannot enter any data, I want to disable the title field on the form. However, whenever I disable the title field on the form, the code runs and I can see the new value entered, but on a reload of the form (after a save), the value returns to its initial state.

```
//script to autopopulate the case title field.

var part1 = crmForm.all.casetypecode.SelectedText;
var part2 = crmForm.all.cf_casesubtype.SelectedText;
var part3 =
crmForm.all.cf_systemorganisation.DataValue;
var part4 = (part1+' - ' + part2 +' - ' + part3);
crmForm.all.title.DataValue = part4;
```

It works fine when the title field is not disabled.

How can I do it?

A: You should set the value for ForceSubmit as well for disabled fields:

```
crmForm.all.title.DataValue = part4;
crmForm.all.title.ForceSubmit = true;
```

Question 24: Field value does not get saved in Database

I have some 'read only' and disabled field but values do not get saved in the database when I save my form.

Why is this?

A: It is because enabled fields will be submitted after they have been modified either through script or by user input. Set this property to 'True' for disabled or read-only fields and for fields that have not been modified if you want to submit them.

You can also use this:

```
crmForm.all.createdon.ForceSubmit = true;
```

Question 25: Custom Fields & Business Required

I created a custom entity and added it as a field to the product form. However, because I made it 'Business required' it will not allow me to remove the field from the form. Going back to the entity itself that attribute is grayed out and unchangeable.

Do I need to make manual changes to the database itself to remove the field?

A: You can change the requirement level through the relationship and set it to 'No Constraint'. Then publish the changes and you should be able to remove the field from the form.

Question 26: Linking fields within the same entity

Is it possible to link fields within the same entity like Opportunity field to Opportunity field e.g. Opportunity Field 1 on Tab 1 needs to populate Opportunity Field 2 on Tab 2?

A: It is not possible to create a new relationship from the same entity except for a few 'System Entities'.

The alternative way is to use some JScript code (On-change or On-save) to copy the value of field on one tab to field on other tab. Try this code in "on-change" event of 'Field1' on 'Tab1' in your opportunity form:

```
crmForm.all.<field2_tab2>.DataValue=crmForm.all.<field1_tab1>.DataValue:
```

```
Here <field1_tab1> is Schema Name of your first field in Tab 1;
```

Question 27: Print out the value of a date/time variable from a query

I have a query that runs fine:

```
QueryExpression myQuery = new QueryExpression();
BusinessEntityCollection roles =
service.RetrieveMultiple(myQuery);
```

I loop thru each entity and retrieve a GUID, a status & a date\time:

```
foreach (new_equipmentreservation newEquip in
roles.BusinessEntities)
{
myLog += ("Reservation GUID=" +
newEquip.new_equipmentreservationid.Value.ToString()
+ " : status=" +
newEquip.statuscode.Value.ToString() + "new_re=" +
newEquip.new_re.Value.ToString() + "\n");
}
```

I can see the GUID & status value, but adding the line to see the date and time causes an error:

"Object reference not set to an instance of an object."

How do I solve this?

A: The newEquip.new_re is null for that record. You may use the following:

```
myLog += ("Reservation GUID=" +
newEquip.new_equipmentreservationid.Value.ToString()
+ " : status=" +
newEquip.statuscode.Value.ToString() + "new_re=" +
(newEquip.new_re == null ? "<null>" :
newEquip.new_re.Value.ToString() +
"\n");
```

Question 28: Making a picklist

I have about 30 checkboxes. A specific number of them make up Package A. Package A plus other specific checkboxes would make up Package B. Package B plus a few other checkboxes would make up Package C.

So, what I wanted to do was make a pick list: Package A, Package B, Package C.

If a user were to select one of the above it would auto check the appropriate check boxes. If they then wanted to add and/or remove check boxes after, that's ok. Its just there to save time by saving clicks.

Can you show me the code to fill in my field name and paste it into onchange?

A: Yes, I can show you how. Your picklist's OnChange event should look like this:

```
var picklistText =
crmForm.all.new_picklist.SelectedText;
var a = (picklistText == "Package A");
var b = (picklistText == "Package B");
var c = (picklistText == "Package C");

//for all checkboxes that should be checked when a is
selected:
crmForm.all.new_checkbox1.DataValue = a;

//for all checkboxes that should be checked when b is
selected:
crmForm.all.new_checkbox1.DataValue = b;

//for all checkboxes that should be checked when a or
b is selected:
crmForm.all.new_checkbox1.DataValue = a || b;
```

And so on. If you include all of your checkboxes like this, they will be reset to the values you want whenever the picklist value changes.

Question 29: Change a value in a field by the selection of the user

I'm new to developing in CRM and I am starting small. All I want to do is change a value in one field on a form depending on a picklist selection the user makes. I've opened the form in the customizations menu and have gone to the scripts tab of the picklist control and entered the following:

```
var oField = crmForm.all.salesstagecode;
var oProbability = crmForm.all.closeprobability;

if (oField.SelectedText = "Opportunity")
{
oProbability.DataValue = 10;
}
else if (oField.SelectedText = "Proposal")
{
oProbability.DataValue = 50;
}
```

The oField picklist contains 5 items. Whenever the user selects an item from it (say the 3rd item), the oProbability field updates properly. However, a side effect of this is that the oField picklist on the form then replaces the 3rd item in its list with the item in the 1st position and only displays the 1st item in the list. It repeats this no matter which item in the list you choose e.g. select item 2 and the picklist will display the item in position 1 and replace the item in position 2 with the item in position 1. Eventually, all the items in the list show item 1 only.

How do I fix this?

A: Comparison in Javascript is ==, not =. Operator = is actually assigning value, so by doing if (oField.SelectedText = "Opportunity"), you actually assign oField.SelectedText to "Opportunity" and this syntax is simply returned 'true'.

So, you use this instead: if (oField.SelectedText == "Opportunity")

Question 30: Independent Fields

Is there anyway to add a field to a form that is not linked to an underlying table field?

For example a calculated field that is filled based on values from two other fields?

A: There is no way to add such fields in the form designer, but you can use an IFRAME displaying the information. Also you can add additional controls at runtime using client-side scripting.

Question 31: Jscript to set a second date field 5 years on from another date field

I am using the following script for an event for an onchange on one field to set a second date field but nothing happens.

My code is below:

```
if(crmForm.all.nswit_pc_achieve_by.DataValue == null)

{
var date.nswit_dateofappointment.datavalue;
date.setYear(date.getYear() + 5);
crmForm.all.nswit_pc_achieve_by.datevalue = date;
}

else {

// do nothing }
```

How do I fix this?

A: You may use this correction:

```
if(crmForm.all.nswit_pc_achieve_by.DataValue == null)
{
var myDate =
crmForm.all.nswit_dateofappointment.DataValue;
myDate.setYear(myDate.getYear() + 5);
crmForm.all.nswit_pc_achieve_by.DataValue = myDate;
}
```

Question 32: Advanced Search in LookUp

LookUp by default can look for text in the principal 'Attribute' of an identity. But I need to search for multiple field examples for 'Name' or 'Address' of a contact. Can it be done with CRM? I need to be sure that I don't have any free way to do this customization with CRM.

A: You will be able to allow your users to search on any number of different field values when they use a lookup field to establish a relationship between records in Microsoft CRM. You will find that it is built in to Microsoft CRM.

If you go to Customization > Customize Entities - then select the entity, let's say Contacts.

Locate the 'Contacts Lookup' view. Open the view and note the "Add Find Columns" button. This button will give you a list of fields that can be searched. By default, only the Name fields (first, middle, last, and full name) are searched. The e-mail field is also searched.

If you want to add more fields like phone numbers, select those fields, save the entity, and publish it. Your users will then be able to search using data in those fields. But they will need to choose a single field to search on. There is no way to include AND or OR logic in the search although they can use the asterisk as a wildcard.

Question 33: Username from userID

I need to get the username having userID in a postcreate callout (C#). I had a look to whoamI but I think that it's useful only if I need to impersonate another user.

Do you know the way to get it?

A: Yes, I do. Use the 'retrieve method' to get the system user object based on the UserID property of the userContext that's passed to the callout.

```
ColumnSet cs = new ColumnSet();
cs.Attributes = new string[] {"fullname"};
systemuser user = (systemuser)
svc.Retrieve("systemuser",
userContext.UserId, cs);
```

Question 34: Forcing a change

I would like to force a change every time an Onload form occurs which will change the modifiedby to the current UserID. So basically, I would like to Onload, maybe have a field called crmForm.all.count.DataValue = # + 1 and then Autosave on an Onload.

Do you have any idea on how to do the jscript for this?

A: In CRM SDK, there is a method call Save or SaveAndClose. Try: crmForm.Save(); in OnLoad method.

Question 35: PartyObjectTypeCode & ParticipationTypeMask

I am looking for resources used for a service appointment.

Do you know what "PartyObjectTypeCode" & "ParticipationTypeMask" do in the "ActivityParty"?

What values should I use for these two (2) fields?

Will "PartyObjectTypeCode = 8" & "ParticipationTypeMask = 10" result in all resources?

A: PartyObjectTypeCode is the type of entity you want to use as a resource. So if you're looking for system user resources, then 8 is fine. However, you can also use 'Equipment' entities as a resource, which would be type 4000.

ParticipationTypeMask specifies the type of Activity Party, so in case of resources for a service appointment, 10 is the one you need.

If you're looking for all resources on a service appointment, you only need to specify the participationtypemask=10.

Question 36: Null in Jscript

I want to autofill Topic and this works, however when
Companyname is null it actually puts a null in the topic.

Is there a way to say if null then don't do it?

```
crmForm.all.address1_county.DataValue = county;
crmForm.all.subject.DataValue = county + ' - '+
crmForm.all.companyname.DataValue +
crmForm.all.lastname.DataValue+', '
+ crmForm.all.firstname.DataValue;
```

A: This is a feature of the HTML controls used in CRM.
Whenever a field is set to an empty value (empty text, unselected
picklist or lookup), the 'Data Value' is null. To avoid seeing the
"null" in the resulting text, you need to wrap your code like the
following:

```
var s1 = (county == null) ? : county;
var s2 = (crmForm.all.companyname.DataValue == null)
? "" :
crmForm.all.companyname.DataValue;
var s3 = (crmForm.all.lastname.DataValue == null) ?
"" :
crmForm.all.lastname.DataValue;
var s4 = (crmForm.all.firstname.DataValue == null) ?
"" :
crmForm.all.firstname.DataValue;

crmForm.all.subject.DataValue = s1 + ' - ' + s2 + s3
+ ', ' + s4;
```

Question 37: Hide or show fields based on picklist

I've managed to hide field on the form based on a picklist selection using this code:

```
if (crmForm.all.ums_currency.value == "2")
{
crmForm.all.ums_totalnoofsubs.style.display = "none";
}
```

The problem is that after picking the value that hides the field I can't show it again. It stays hidden even if I change the chosen value.

How do I show it again?

A: You can use the following to show/hide fields dynamically:

```
if (crmForm.all.ums_currency.value == "2") {
//hide the field
crmForm.all.ums_totalnoofsubs.style.display = "none";
}

else {
//show the field
crmForm.all.ums_totalnoofsubs.style.display = "";
}
```

Question 38: Removing one access right from Access Mask

I have an existing 'Access Mask' from which I would like to remove one particular 'Access Right'.

An example is as follows:

Existing:
```
ReadAccess | WriteAccess | AppendAccess |
AppendToAccess | CreateAccess |
DeleteAccess | ShareAccess | AssignAccess
```

And now I want to remove 'ShareAccess'

Target:
```
ReadAccess | WriteAccess | AppendAccess |
AppendToAccess | CreateAccess |
DeleteAccess | AssignAccess
```

Is there a way I can remove only one Access Right from this mask or do I have to create a function, which (for example) goes through all existing entries and creates a new mask, but without the one Access Right I want to remove?

A: You can do by the following:

```
AccessRights existing = AccessRights.ReadAccess |
AccessRights.WriteAccess |
AccessRights.AppendAccess | ...

AccessRights target = existing &
~AccessRights.ShareAccess;
```

Question 39: Convert businessEntityCollection to Dynamic Entity

I was trying this:

```
BusinessEntityCollection retrieved =
service.RetrieveMultiple(query);
if (retrieved.BusinessEntities.Length > 0)
{
for (int i = 0; i <
retrieved.BusinessEntities.Length; i++)
{
DynamicEntity entity =
(DynamicEntity)retrieved.BusinessEntities[i];
}
}
```

But this will give an error at runtime: "The conversion is not valid." How do I convert a BusinessEntityCollection to a DynamicEntity? How do I fill a ColumnSet with dynamic fields? For example:

```
string attributes = String.Format("{0}, {1}, {2}",
keyField.toString(),
guidFieldBase.toString(), fieldNameBase.toString());
cols.Attributes = new string []
{attributes.toString};
```

A: To retrieve dynamic entities, you need to set the ReturnDynamicEntitites flag in the RetrieveMultipleRequest:

```
RetrieveMultipleRequest request = new
RetrieveMultipleRequest();
request.Query = query;
request.ReturnDynamicEntities = true;

RetrieveMultipleRespones response =
service.Execute(request);
```

To set a list of attributes, do the following:

```
cols.Attributes = new string [] {keyField,
guidFieldBase, fieldNameBase};
```

Question 40: Link to file in an IFRAME

Is it possible to create a link towards a file that contains files relating to an opportunity?

Those files should be showed in an IFRAME (named: IFRAME_Offre). I tried to do like in the "Simple IFRAME Question" subject but it doesn't work. I wish to show files instead of web site. If I type the access path in the URL IFRAME field: it's ok. But I wish that this access path came from another field (named: DossierOffre) that will be recorded during the creation of the form.

A: Yes it is. You need to set the Iframe src property in your onload event, like:

```
if (crmForm.all.DossierOffre.DataValue != null) {
crmForm.all.IFRAME_Offre.src =
crmForm.all.DossierOffre.DataValue;
}
```

Set the default url to about:blank. The DossierOffre field should contain a link to a folder in unc format, say \\fileserver\opportunities\opportunity name. You need to set appropriate file security on the directory and the share, but in my environment it does work. You also need to add the CRM server to the list of trusted sites in IE to avoid security warnings when trying to access the files in the file share.

Question 41: Onsave javascript event, exit without saving

I have quite a complex IS script on one of my form. I would like to check that all the fields have been filled correctly on the Onsave event. If one is not correct I want the user to be unable to save. There is a callout that is triggering something else.

To sum up, in the onsave event, I would like to be able to exit without saving.

Is there a function to do this?

A: Yes. Look at the OnSave sample in the sdk - that is what the documentation is for.

```
var CRM_FORM_SAVE_MODE_SAVE = 1;
var CRM_FORM_SAVE_MODE_SAVEANDCLOSE = 2;

// Validate only if the user clicked "Save".
switch (event.Mode)
{
case CRM_FORM_SAVE_MODE_SAVE:

// If the user provided a first and last name, they
//must provide a job title as well.
if (crmForm.all.jobtitle.DataValue == "" &&
crmForm.all.firstname.DataValue != "" &&
crmForm.all.lastname.DataValue != "" &&
{
// Tell the user what is wrong.
alert("Please provide a Job Title for this person.");

// Give the control focus.
crmForm.all.jobtitle.SetFocus();

// Cancel the save operation.
event.returnValue = false;
return false;
}

break;

case CRM_FORM_SAVE_MODE_SAVEANDCLOSE:
// If the user forgot to provide a job title, set a
//default title.
if (crmForm.all.jobtitle.DataValue == "")
{
```

```
// Set a default Job Title.
crmForm.all.jobtitle.DataValue = "N/A";

//Because this is a "Save and Close", just save the
//form.
return true;
}

break;
}
```

Question 42: Putting calculations into fields of the 'Opportunities' entity

I need to be able to put calculations into the fields of the 'opportunities' entity. For example, I want a field to take a percentage of another field or one field be the sum of two other fields.

How can I do this?

Is JavaScript necessary?

A: You can use JavaScript by putting it in the right event. You could use the OnSave() event handler of the form to calculate your values. You can access to fields' values using:

```
"crmForm.all.FIELD_NAME.DataValue"

where FIELD_NAME is the attribute schema name;
```

Question 43: Auto fill fields in custom entity

I have a custom entity that I've set up, complete with lookup mappings to Account. However, in the custom entity I also have the 'Account Name' field and would like the field to be automatically completed once the 'Account Number' is selected.

Is there an easy way to do this?

A: Yes. This can be done with some simple JavaScript in the Onchange event on the 'Account Lookup' field.

Something like this will work just fine:

```
if(crmForm.all.new_accountid.DataValue.length > 0)
{
crmForm.all.new_accountname.DataValue =
crmForm.all.new_accountid.DataValue[0].name;
}
```

Question 44: Hiding fields on forms

I am part of a team implementing Ms CRM 3.0 in an environment where many fields need to be hidden and revealed or deactivated according to a property of the record. My teammate has this feature working very well.

However, there seem to be some oddities with hiding/deactivating date/time fields. The field is hidden, but not the calendar control, which still works, and will set a date into an otherwise invisible field.

What is the most possible way to accomplish this?

A: There are a couple of elements you can hide, taking the lastusedincampaign as a sample:

```
lastusedincampaign_c - the label
lastusedincampaign_d - the control
lastusedincampaign - the date/time textbox
lastusedincampaignimg - the image (magnifying glass)
```

Hiding lastusedincampaign_c and lastusedincampaign_d should hide the entire control. If you currently only hide lastusedincampaign, the image will not be affected.

Question 45: Custom Entity Script Error

I'm building my first custom entity and ran into a problem. I am trying to pre-populate a field after filling either one of these two fields: new_publicationid is a lookup with Products and new_advertiserid is a lookup with Accounts. I want to concatenate the Product, Account and DateTime to be a proxy for a GUID. It is not the best solution, but its all I know to do. I get an error with the following script when the new_advertiserid is empty.

```
var vDate = String(new Date());
var vPubID = String(new Date());
var vAdvID = String(new Date());

if (crmForm.all.new_publicationid.DataValue[0].id !=
null)
{
vPubID =
crmForm.all.new_publicationid.DataValue[0].id;
}
if (crmForm.all.new_advertiserid.DataValue[0].id !=
null)
{
vAdvID =
crmForm.all.new_advertiserid.DataValue[0].id;

}
crmForm.all.new_name.DataValue = String(vPubID) +
String(vAdvID) +
String(vDate);
```

What am I doing wrong?

A: You need to check if crmForm.all.new_advertiserid.DataValue is null, before accessing a member of the array. The same is true for new_publicationid:

```
if (crmForm.all.new_publicationid.DataValue != null)
{
vPubID =
crmForm.all.new_publicationid.DataValue[0].id;
}
```

Question 46: Populate multiple fields with one lookup

I'd like to populate multiple fields with one lookup. I have a new entity "zipcodes" linked to the company entity. The zipcode entity holds the matching ZIP and city information. The initial update of the city field I do with a workflow triggered on the create event of the company entity.

What can I do to keep it up to date?

Is there a possibility to 'read' fields of joined entities in the OnChange event?

A: The only way to maintain this would be to use a callout to keep the city names in sync when they are updated in the zipcodes table. One thing to watch out for though is that there are areas where the same zip code is used for multiple cities, so you could run into problems with this design.

Question 47: Deactivate custom entity

I want to deactivate custom entity from the code but I receive a "Server was unable to process request" error message. The entity's name is 'MyCustomObject'. Everything else in the code seems to be working fine. For example, I can retrieve entity and update some other fields like 'name', etc. However, for some reason, I can't deactivate it.

```
. . .
//this doesn't produce any errors, but nothing
happens when I set
'statecode' alone
New_MyCustomObjectStateInfo stateInfo = new
New_MyCustomObjectStateInfo();
stateInfo.Value = New_MyCustomObjectState.Inactive;
mycustomobject.statecode = stateInfo;

// this is what seems to be causing errors when I set
'status' to the code:
Status status = new Status();
status.Value = 2;
mycustomobject.statuscode = status;
. . .
```

It seems that I'm missing some correct syntax and/or correct approach to this case.

Looking at the MetaData browser shows this for my custom entity:

```
statecode no (ValidForCreate) yes (Valid for Read) no
(Valid for Update)
statuscode yes (ValidForCreate) yes (Valid for Read)
yes (Valid for Update)
```

It doesn't seem like it has anything to do with my problem because 'statecode' doesn't throw errors on update, and it has a value of 'no' for 'Valid for Update' field.

What am I missing here?

A: You need to use: SetStateMyCustomObjectRequest.

Question 48: Relationships in CRM

We have created several custom entities in order to achieve the registration of order and supplies in a different way than CRM Order default. We did this through the creation of the following:

1. Entity with Order Data (Account - Order ID - Order Date).
2. Entity for product details like text for product description and field which calculate price depending on quantities, tax etc.

I created a relationship and mapping for Order ID and account, and that the problem is we need a lookup field in order to indicate the supplier for the product. We think suppliers are seen as accounts in CRM so we can't create a second relationship (Accounts-Product Details Custom Entity) and get the supplier account.

What could we do to accomplish this?

A: At a basic level you can simply expose a text field and manually type the name of the supplier in a more sophisticated approach, although not necessarily the most logical for end users, is to do the following:

1. Create a new custom entity named suppliers.
2. Link this entity to accounts and then create a new many to one relationship from suppliers to accounts.
3. On the new supplier entity form expose the attribute for accounts.
4. On your custom order entity create a new many to one relationship with supplier.
5. On your custom order form expose the new relationship attribute.

It means an additional mouse click but achieves what you require by simply creating a new entity to 'bridge' your custom orders and accounts with a new supplier entity.

Question 49: Creating relationship to Contract Lines

I have created a custom entity for subcontractors and I want to add a relationship from the Contract Lines entity to subcontractors like in service to allow the lookup of the subcontractor from a contract line. I can add a relationship to the Contract entity but not to Contract Lines.

How can I do this?

A: The reason you can't do this is that Contract Line is not a user owned entity. Contract line is kind of unique. Most entities are 'user-owned', 'organization-owned', and a few are 'business unit-owned'. The ownership is important because it controls how cascading actions might occur. I don't know the details about why contract line is not user owned and 'Contract' is. But I expect that the contract line is supposed to be associated with the Contract so it is essentially 'contract owned'.

Bottom line is, there is no way to create a CRM relationship between contract line and a custom entity.

Here are some other options:

Use an IFrame in the ContractLine form which displays a custom page that does a lookup on your custom entity. Create custom attributes on the Contractline form. When the user saves the form, update the entity with values taken from the IFrame. This will require some development effort.

If your list of subcontractors is short and doesn't change much, you might configure them as a picklist in the contractline form. I wouldn't recommend this if you have a very long list (100+) and maintaining a list of valid subcontractors would need to be done manually.

Question 50: Setting a URL dynamically

I would like to be able to integrate an iFrame within an entity so that it points to a related document specific to an instance of that entity.

How do I construct the URL so that it is composed with parameters specific to that entity?

A: If the data you need is available on the form, you can pull it with jscript and format the URL with querystring parms and then set the target URL of the iFRame.

Question 51: Subject entity metadata

I need to populate a web form and give the user a list of 'Incident' subjects to select from when they raise a case. I have no problem getting the entity data for picklists, etc. but cannot get a handle on the Subject entity.

Here is an example of the code I am using to retrieve attribute data via the metadata web service and adding the data to an asp.net drop down list control:

```
Dim oMetaDataService As crmMetadata.MetadataService =
oCRM.MetaDataService
Dim oAttributeMetaData As
crmMetadata.AttributeMetadata

'Get list info for Case Type
oAttributeMetaData =
oMetaDataService.RetrieveAttributeMetadata("incident"
, "casetypecode")
Dim PickList As crmMetadata.PicklistAttributeMetadata
PickList = CType(oAttributeMetaData,
crmMetadata.PicklistAttributeMetadata)
Dim oOption As crmMetadata.Option
For Each oOption In PickList.Options
Dim oListItem As New ListItem
oListItem.Value = oOption.OptionValue
oListItem.Text = oOption.Description
lstNewComplaintCaseType.Items.Add(oListItem)
Next
--
```

How can I retrieve the 'Subject' entity metadata via the CRM web services?

A: The subjects are not stored in the metabase. Use CrmService.RetrieveMultiple instead, to retrieve the list of possible values.

Question 52: Change name of Opportunities

Is it possible to change the name of the entities listed under Sales, Marketing and Service?

A: Yes. Open the entity in settings/customization and specify the new name. Save and publish your changes. If you don't see the new name in your browser, hit F5 or CTRL-F5 to refresh it. The new entity name should be present in all areas, including buttons, menus and the navigation bars.

Question 53: Copy Contact name to a text box

I'd really like to be able to put the full name of a contact or company into a text box in a related entities form. An example of this would be an onSave event in a custom entities form, after the user has selected a contact or company from a lookup field. I'd like the text of the value displayed in the lookup field to be copied and pasted into another field on the same form.

Is this possible?

A: Yes, this is possible. In the OnChange event of the lookup field put the following code:

```
if (crmForm.all.<lookupField>.DataValue == null) {
crmForm.all.<textField>.DataValue = null;
}

else {
crmForm.all.<textField>.DataValue =
crmForm.all.<lookupField>.DataValue[0].name;
}
```

Question 54: Full Entity XSD Schema

When you query a CRM entity using FetchXML, you get XML returned to you. If you look at that XML, it has all the fields from the entity as XML nodes, but it also has attributes on these nodes.

For example:

```
<field1 attribute1="" attribute2=""
attribute3="">value</field1>
```

I would like to know what XML attributes are returned for each field. I have been doing a FetchXML query and looking at the XML, but it would be nice if there was just something I could look at to verify this.

Is there some documentation that shows the full entity XSD schema?

A: The additional attributes are specific to the attribute type and correspond to the virtual fields you see in the metadata. Some examples are as follows:

Picklist field: contains the option value (integer) in the inner text plus the name attribute, which is the textual representation.

Boolean field: contains 0 or 1 in the inner text plus the name attribute, which is the textual representation (like "No" or "False").

Date Fields: contains the date in the inner text plus the date and time attributes, holding the formatted values.

Reference fields (Lookup, Owner, Customer): contains the Guid in the inner text and optional attributes like type (referenced entity type), name (display name of referenced entity), dsc (deletion state code)
And so on.

I don't know if there is a formal specification out there. The easiest way is to look at the Property classes, as they contain the same fields, for example:

```
Lookup class, derived from CrmReference.

class CrmReference {
int dsc;
bool dscSpecified;
bool IsNull;
bool IsNullSpecified;
string name;
string type;
bool Value
}
```

It seems that all properties starting with a lowercase character are returned (or may be returned) as attributes. An exception is dscSpecified, as this in input parameter.

Question 55: Adding navigation bar to the setting area

I am able to add custom navigation bar to specific entities. But now I need to add custom navigation bar to the root like Settings or Workplace.

How can I do this to the Settings area?

A: You need to edit the Sitemap for this. Do it by exporting the Sitemap entity (settings, customization, and export customizations), making a copy for backup purposes, editing and then importing. The CRM SDK has documentation about editing the content.

Question 56: Relate a custom entity with several entities

I have a custom entity, event, and I have created a relationship with the Contact entity. I was just wandering how to modify this relationship so that the field that holds the foreign key could relate either to a contact, an account or a lead.

The example could be the 'to field' of a Phone Call, that can be Account, Lead, Contact or User.

How can I do this?

A: The CRM does not support the kind of relationship you described for custom entities. A special case is the 'parent customer' field of the contact entity, which is such a relationship but is realized through a special code by Microsoft.

However, you can realize such relationships by creating a text field that contains the id of the referenced entity and another one that contains the type of the entity. But you need to implement the whole selection behavior yourself. You need to modify the UI and include another website through an iframe and so on. However, the advanced search would not work on an extension like that.

Question 57: Search for a product based entity with another field

Do you know how to search for a 'Product' based entity through another field besides name-like code, for example?

The idea is, under a form, to search for a product with either Name or Code. Under Advanced Search, I tried to let two (2) conditions, grouped by OR, but they ask for a value.

A: You may go this way:

Customization, Customize Entities, Product entity, Form and views, Products Lookup view, then Add Find Columns to add other columns.;

Remember to save and publish the form.

Question 58: Adding script to OnChange event

I need to add some script into event OnChange of scheduledend and scheduledstart from the appointment form. These attributes are in the appointment form and inside a locked section. Hence, I cannot add any script.

How can I accomplish this ?

A: You can add something similar to the following into the OnLoad form event:

```
crmForm.all.scheduledend.onchange = function() {
alert("Your function here");
}
```

However, this will probably not help you, as locked fields do not trigger their OnChange functions. This is due to the fact that form fields do not trigger their OnChange function unless they were manually changed by a user.

Question 59: Deleting 1.2 custom attributes after upgrade to 3.0

We have a lot of custom attributes in 1.2 that are not being used and will still not be used after we move to 3.0.

Our consulting partner wants us to upgrade and not do a migration of 1.2 data but does not have an answer to the question of deleting the custom columns upgraded from 1.2.

We understand it will take longer and therefore cost more money to migrate data rather than just doing an upgrade but we do not want these columns in 3.0.

Can these custom attributes be deleted once they are in 3.0?

A: Yes, you can delete the 1.2 custom attributes after the upgrade from CRM 1.2 to 3.0.

Question 60: Call an attribute from Form

I created a new attribute in the Product entity; let's name it statusprod. This attribute is a pick list with 2 values. When you create a product, you select "Available" as a value for statusprod. Then, when the product is sold, you modify the statusprod to "Sold".

Now, I want to create an 'Opportunity' and add a 'New Opportunity Product'.

What can I do to get an alert when I select a product with the "Sold" statusprod or even to hide the products with the "Sold" statusprod?

Can you post some code for this please?

A: You can use a built-in status attribute of 'Product'.

Activate: Available
Sold: Deactivate.

You can set this status from Action menu in the 'Product's Form'.

Question 61: Linking Attributes on Lead Screen

Can you point me in the direction of where or how attributes and fields on the lead screen can be converted to the Account, Contact and Opportunity screens?

A: You may open the entity in the edit mode, open "relationship", and finally, in this list open LEAD / CONTACT.

In the next window you can set the attributes, which will be used to change a lead in a contact.

Question 62: Show Same Attribute on Multiple Tabs of same Form

I have a situation where I would like to show the 'Social Security Number' attribute on two (2) different tabs on the Account form. In the form editor, once I place the attribute on a tab, that attribute gets removed from the picklist, so I can't pick it a second time to put it on an additional tab.

Can I solve this with JavaScript and DHTML by adding the attribute on the tab with the form's OnLoad event?

A: Yes, you can do that. Using JavaScript you have to create a text box element or you can take the inner HTML and put in the next tab. It will require time and good knowledge of JavaScript.

You can do one more thing. If you change the value in text box of CRM, it will automatically fill the value of that text box.

Question 63: Bulk reassignment of account owner in CRM

We have just let a salesperson go and wish to reassign his accounts. There are around 500 of these so we would like to do this in bulk if possible. I cannot see how to do this easily.

What is the best way to accomplish this task?

A: You may use 'advanced find' function to isolate the accounts where owner = GuyWhoLeft. Then select all with shift-click, then click 'Assign' button on the button bar.

An alternative course of action is this: when someone leaves your company you should go into their CRM user record then click on actions-reassign records and choose another user to reassign their records to. At this point you can then disable their record to release the license.

Question 64: Passing AccountID to a custom web application

I am new to CRM and I want to know if this is possible. I have created a navigation button in isv.config and try to pass the active AccountID to my web application so I can get the information for this customer from the CRM database.

How can I pass an AccountID or customer id to my web application?

A: In the XML, for your new button in the isv.config, add the PassParams="1" attribute. This will add an "oid={......}" to the querystring in the call to your web page. The ID inside the {} will be the AccountID of the currently selected account.

Question 65: Creating invoice by the post create opportunity

I am trying to create an invoice by the 'postcreate' of opportunity.

In the code I incorporated this:

```
invoice inv=new invoice();
inv.cuatomerId=.......(how can I assign a xml value
from the postImageEntityXml to it?)
same as inv.opportunityId=........
```

Am I doing the right thing?

A: The xml that you get is a serialized bag of opportunity entity. Follow these steps and you should be able to get the correct values:

1. Add the entries to the callout.config.xml so that you get post values in the Xml.
2. Parse the Xml to read the required values. You could use Xpath to find them. I have provided a version that is in sync with documentation.
3. Then you can use the values easily.

```
<callout entity="opportunity" event="PostCreate">
<subscription assembly="Callout1.dll"
class="CalloutAssembly.CreateOpportunity">
<postvalue>@all</postvalue>
</subscription>
</callout>

public override void PostCreate(CalloutUserContext
userContext,
CalloutEntityContext entityContext, string
postImageEntityXml)
{
string attributeValue = null;
string oppid =
OppCreate.GetPropertyValue("opportunityid", null,
postImageEntityXml, out attributeValue);
// attributeValue now has the type of the entity as
account or contact
string custid =
OppCreate.GetPropertyValue("customerid", "type",
postImageEntityXml, out attributeValue);
}
```

```
static string GetPropertyValue(string propertyName,
string attributeName,
string imageXml, out string attributeNameValue)
{
attributeNameValue = null;
NameTable nt = new NameTable();
// Initialize a namespace manager.
XmlNamespaceManager nsmgr = new
XmlNamespaceManager(nt);

// Add the required prefix/namespace pairs to the
namespace
// manager. Add a default namespace first.
nsmgr.AddNamespace("crm",
"http://schemas.microsoft.com/crm/2006/WebServices");
nsmgr.AddNamespace("xsi",
"http://www.w3.org/2001/XMLSchema-instance");

XmlDocument d = new XmlDocument();
d.LoadXml(imageXml);
XmlNode n =
d.SelectSingleNode(".//crm:Property[@Name='" +
propertyName +
"']/crm:Value",nsmgr);
if (n != null)
{
if (attributeName != null)
{
XmlNode custType =
n.Attributes.GetNamedItem(attributeName);
if (custType != null)
{
attributeNameValue = custType.InnerText;
}
}
return n.InnerText;
}
return null;
}
```

Question 66: New account in CRM

If one creates a new account in CRM, should it trigger PostCreate events for both the account itself and its Address 1, given that address information has been typed?

I have written two callouts, one for accounts and one for addresses. If I create an additional address for an account, the address PostCreate callout is executed. However, for some reason that callout is not executed when I create a new account with the basic address information.

Why does this happen?

A: All the fields on all the tabs on Account form are part of Account entity. Address 1 and Address 2 are created by default with account even if you don't put any information in their fields. Address 1 and 2 are part of the Account so any update on them in Account form will be update to Account and so Account callouts will be called. If you create any new address, then only address callout will be called. So the behavior you are experiencing is fine.

Question 67: Get parent ObjectId from IFRAME in Create form

I have some custom attributes for Account, CustomerAddress, and Contact that require special user interface components for entry. I have the UI for these attributes in an IFRAME and can successfully save the values in my asp.net pages that are hosted in them. Unfortunately, it only works for Update forms, because the ObjectId doesn't appear to be available to the IFRAMEs when saving from a Create form.

I'm wondering where in the save process the form OnSave gets fired. It seems to be before the actual Save of the form, since the ObjectId isn't populated before the form is reloaded.

Is there a way to deal with this?

A: You're right. The OnSave method is called before the entity is saved to the database. This is correct because otherwise you wouldn't have the chance to cancel the save operation. After OnSave finishes, the data is sent to the server and any pre-create callout may decide to reject it. Therefore, even after OnSave is finished, there's no guarantee that the data is saved.

All in all, there's no way to get to the crmForm.ObjectId in a create form.

Question 68: Callout on account sharing

I want to send email to user when any account gets share with user.

Which entity is used in callout for this purpose?

A: 'Share' is not supported in callouts. Only 'Assign' is the closest but 'Assign' changes the ownership rather than working on sharing the access to the user record.

Question 69: Error in creating a new contractdetail

I'm trying to create a new contract detail using an assembly. For the sake of testing, I'm hard-coding the Product and UoM. When I try to create the contract detail, it throws a Soap error and cannot create the object.

Here is the code I am trying to run. 'myContract' is a valid contract entity which I retrieved elsewhere.

```
Dim myDetail As New contractdetail
myDetail.price = New CrmMoney
myDetail.price.Value = 1.0

myDetail.totalallotments = New CrmNumber
myDetail.totalallotments.Value = 1

myDetail.activeon = New CrmDateTime
myDetail.activeon.Value = CDate(Now)
myDetail.expireson = New CrmDateTime
myDetail.expireson.Value =
CDate(DateAdd(DateInterval.Year, 1, Now))

myDetail.customerid = New Customer
myDetail.customerid.type = myContract.customerid.type
myDetail.customerid.Value =
myContract.customerid.Value

myDetail.title = "Dummy Item"
myDetail.contractid = New Lookup
myDetail.contractid.type = EntityName.contract
myDetail.contractid.Value =
myContract.contractid.Value

myDetail.productid = New Lookup
myDetail.productid.type = EntityName.product
myDetail.productid.Value = New
Guid("F1264662-CEC1-DB11-8FA2-000BCD4E15CC")

myDetail.uomid = New Lookup
myDetail.uomid.type = EntityName.uom
myDetail.uomid.Value = New
Guid("351F26B5-9D4C-DB11-A442-000BCD4E15CC")

Dim userRequest As New WhoAmIRequest
Dim user As WhoAmIResponse =
CType(service.Execute(userRequest),
WhoAmIResponse)

myDetail.owninguser = New UniqueIdentifier
```

```
myDetail.owninguser.Value = user.UserId
service.Create(myDetail)
```

I've checked through the contract detail list and included all of the attributes that it claims are required. The SDK documentation, however, seems to contradict the list, claiming that contract id is not valid for 'create' purposes. I'm assuming creating a contract detail through code is possible.

Any ideas what may be wrong?

A: Did you trap the SoapException and look into the details of that message to see what error is being returned? Perhaps one of the GUIDs you are setting is not valid. I would recommend creating a detail record manually via the UI that contains the same values and then looking at the Contract Detail Base table to see the actual underlying values and try replicating those same values. Also, the WhoAmI call and setting 'Owner' are not needed. 'Owner' will default to the logged in user.

Question 70: Callout Procedures

Basically, on the server we have a directory for each of our accounts that we store certain information in. I've created an Iframe in the account form that points to this directory for each customer for easy access to it. Right now, it is working perfectly.

Is it possible to use Callouts to automatically create the folder on the server (same as the CRM) for the account and the time the account is created?

A: Yes, it is possible. For as long as the file security allows it, your callout can do anything you would like it to do. An alternative method or approach is to do a custom workflow assembly. You can then specify your root directory and account directory in a workflow, which you may find easier to maintain and test as a callout.

Question 71: Add Account to Marketing List Programmatically

How do we use the SDK to add an account or a contact to a Marketing List?

I see no properties or methods on the Account or List class that ties them to each other so I presume it is a third class or other request mechanism. However, I can't find any documentation or examples anywhere.

A: As there is a many to many relationship between marketing lists and account/contacts, CRM keeps an internal table to store the associations. Use AddMemberListRequest and RemoveMemberListRequest to manage them.

Question 72: Relate multiple users to an account

Our current system is getting prepared for an upgrade from 1.2 to 3.0, W2003, SQL 2000.

We have five (5) "Sales" types of users for each account: Equipment Sales, Network Sales, Supply Sales, Graphics Sales, and Print Sales.

Currently each sales type has a specific and distinct set of users to assign from, that is, and a user is not assigned to more than one sales type. However, we need to be able to do that, just in case.

The way this was setup in 1.2 was scenario wherein there is a custom variable character attribute for each 'Sales Type' and the user name was manually entered and changed. I have seen the last name of one user that is four (4) letters long, with four (4) different spellings.

We need a way to pull the user name from the database and assign them to the appropriate 'Sales Team'. This will not have to be a custom attribute on the Account Entity, we would be quite happy if it was a custom entity associated with the 'Account'.

Is there a simple way to do this or do we need to call in a CRM .NET programmer?

A: This isn't easy to do and isn't particularly clean. Effectively you need to associate multiple users to a single account. We have done something for a client who has many account managers per account. To do this we created a new entity called account manager which is related to both the user and account. This allows you to create multiple account managers per account and assign each one to a user record. We had no need to check for type of user or anything like that, so it depends on how robust it needs to be, or if it can rely on users being sensible. We needed workflow to email all the account managers of an account in certain circumstances. Workflow can only email the owner, and thus we still ended up using custom .net code to do this.

Question 73: Retrieve Contacts by Account ID

I want to retrieve contacts based on an accountID. I am coding in C# and am able to retrieve the contacts and 'Accounts' but I want to get all contacts based on an accountID.

How can I fulfill this?

A: You can fulfill this by a little modification in the function below:

```
/// <summary>
/// This methods checks whether the account given has
one or more sub
contacts.
/// </summary>
/// <param name="AccountId">Account Id</param>
/// <returns>True/False</returns>
private bool AccountHasContacts(Guid AccountId)
{
CrmService service = new CrmService();
service.Credentials =
System.Net.CredentialCache.DefaultCredentials;

Lookup account = new Lookup();
account.type = EntityName.account.ToString();
account.Value = AccountId;

// Create a column set that holds the names of the
columns
// to be retrieved.
ColumnSet colsContact = new ColumnSet();
colsContact.Attributes = new string [] {"fullname",
"contactid"};
// Create the ConditionExpression.
ConditionExpression conditionContact = new
ConditionExpression();

// Set the ConditionExpressions Properties so that
the condition is
// true when the accountid or the contact is equal to
accountId.
conditionContact.AttributeName = "accountid";
conditionContact.Operator = ConditionOperator.Equal;
conditionContact.Values = new string []
{AccountId.ToString()};

// Create the FilterExpression.
```

```
FilterExpression filterContact = new
FilterExpression();

// Set the properties of the FilterExpression.
filterContact.FilterOperator = LogicalOperator.And;
filterContact.Conditions = new ConditionExpression[]
{conditionContact};

// Create the QueryExpression.
QueryExpression queryContact = new QueryExpression();

// Set the properties of the QueryExpression.
queryContact.EntityName =
EntityName.contact.ToString();
queryContact.ColumnSet = colsContact;
queryContact.Criteria = filterContact;

// Retrieve the contacts.
BusinessEntityCollection contacts =
service.RetrieveMultiple(queryContact);
if(contacts.BusinessEntities.Length > 0)
{
return true;
}
else
{
return false;
}
}
}
```

Question 74: Determine any data change in OnSave event

I'd like to run some client side code, but only if the data has changed, and not anytime a user clicks 'save and close'.

Is there a way to determine if any data has changed while at the OnSave event?

A: Yes, there is a way. You may use the following code:

```
var oField = crmForm.all.SOME_FIELD_ID;

if (oField.IsDirty)
{
alert("The field's value has changed.");
}
else
{
alert("The field's value has not changed.");
}
```

Or you can use: CRMForm.IsDirty to provide the information you need.

Customize, Synchronize, Syntax, Cases, Lead Issues

Question 75: Fresh install - Page not found

I just installed CRM 3.0. SQL checks out, I can see the tables. When I type \\localhost\crm, \\localhost\5555, \\localhost, etc. I get a "Page Not Found" error.

Did I miss something?

A: If you took the option 'Create new web site' during the install, the URL when running on the server will be as follows:

http://localhost:5555

or:

https://localhost:5555 if you have SSL;

Question 76: Source Import File is damaged

Why do I get this message, "Source Input File is Damaged" when I try to import customer data?

A: In my experience, I got this error when I had carriage return and linefeed characters in an address field. If you are importing from a file that stored addresses in block format you may have this problem. I had to open the import file in Excel and search that field. I also wrote a crystal report and searched that field for CHR(13) or CHR(10).

Question 77: MSCRM3.0 CDF DTS transformation problem

I try to populate cdf_Lead by using SQL DTS from other data sources but the process failed. You can read the error message on the end of message. It seems like I have to give the LeadID into the record. Will the ID be automatically generated during the insertion or is there something I have to do first before executing the transformation?

Package Name: LEAD
Package Description: (null)
Package ID: {14CE9F51-BF35-48EA-85D9-C6B347CBE1F1}
Package Version: {C48B0A3D-EC40-41B6-A36D-8A9E33C232F5}
Step Name: DTSStep_DTSDataPumpTask_1
Execution Started: 10/20/2006 5:49:22 PM
Error at Destination for Row number 1991. Errors encountered so far in this
task: 1.

Error Source: Microsoft OLE DB Provider for SQL Server
Error Description:The statement has been terminated.
Error Help File:
Error Help Context ID:0

Error Source: Microsoft OLE DB Provider for SQL Server
Error Description:Cannot insert the value NULL into column 'LeadId', table
'cdf_mscrm.dbo.cdf_Lead'; column does not allow nulls.
INSERT fails.
Error Help File:
Error Help Context ID:0

A: The CDF expects you to put something in the LeadID column. Since it is a primary key, you should try creating a column with in the numbers (1,2,3,4...) and import them with the DTS into the LeadID field. Later, when you run the wizard to import the data from CDF into CRM, the wizard will create the GUID which CRM uses as the LeadID.

Question 78: Customizing the Activities View

I'd like to add the contact name and phone number against 'Activities'.

Is it possible to customize 'Activities' and then show it in a list view?

A: Although the activities view is customizable, it can only show fields that are common across all activity types (email, task, appointment etc.), so it cannot show a phone number, as this field is part of the contact.

The contact name will show in the regarding field if set appropriately, but this is not useful for certain activity types (e.g. email, where the contact will normally be in the 'To' or 'From' field).

Question 79: Case form not listed in object publisher

I have done customizations to the case form and saved the customizations. Then, I go into deployment manager, choose all tasks, and then choose publish customizations. At this point I am looking down the list to select the case form to be published. However, it is not listed.

Do you know why I would experience these and how can I go about getting my customizations published?

A: You can look for the 'Incident' list. The name was changed late in the development cycle and it didn't get changed everywhere automatically.

Question 80: Contact Form customization fails

I customized the contacts form. The adjustments appear ok in the system customization view but when I go to the contacts view itself (adding/viewing actual contacts) the unadjusted view still appears.

Is there an extra step involved to activate the change?

A: Yes, you have to deploy your changes, from the CRM deployment manager. Right-click on Deployment manager node, then click "All tasks", then choose the last one: Publish personalization.

Question 81: Generate New Task via Toolbar Button

I know that CRM can be customized to do a lot of things. I want to have an idea on how long it would take to do the following:

A user is viewing a contact record. They would like to be able to hit a toolbar button or menu option to automatically generate a task due in 25 days to visit that contact. The user does not want to do anything other than click the button and the date would automatically be 25 days from today. Maybe a 'confirm' button in case the button was accidentally clicked.

How long would it take to set something like this up assuming it is possible to do?

A: This can be done easily using a web service code running on the CRM server. The button will take the current contact GUID and pass this to a web service, which in turn can create a task with appropriate values. I've done recently similar stuff and it was not that difficult. You can quickly write this within a day or two using SDK and tools.

Question 82: ISV.config file doesn't import

We have recently re-installed CRM to version 3.0.5, and the isv.config customization doesn't seem to work as it used to. Instead, I see an isv.config.xsd schema file where the isv.config.xml file used to be. ISV is set to 'All' in web.config, and when trying to import the following file, it gives an error on line 1, position 2:

```
<configuration
xmlns:xsi="http://www.w3.org/2001/XMLSchema-instance"
xsi:noNamespaceSchemaLocation="C:\Program
Files\Microsoft CRM\CRMWeb\_Resources\isv.config.xsd"
version="3.0.0000.0">

<Root>

<MenuBar>

<CustomMenus>

<Menu Title="Data">

<MenuItem Title="Import"
Url="http://srichdb01:5555/protocol/import.aspx"
WinMode="2" />
<MenuItem Title="Export"
Url="http://srichdb01:5555/protocol/export.aspx"
WinMode="2" />

</Menu>

<Menu Title="Reporting">
<MenuItem Title="Dynamic Report"
Url="http://srichdb01:5555/protocol/dynamicreport.htm
" WinMode="2"/>

</Menu>

</CustomMenus>

</MenuBar>

</Root>

</configuration>
```
How can I fix this?

A: Just copy your isv.config.xml file to _Resource folder and then refresh your CRM to check if changes effects or not. 'isv.config.xsd' is not a customization file but a XML Schema Definition file.

Question 83: Auto Numbering Generates Unique Values

When we create new quote/contract/case/queue, CRM generates auto numbering for each record. When we create two records in cases, the suffix value of auto numbering is completely different. We are not able to identify the relation between the two records.

Why does auto numbering generates number in random order instead of sequence?

A: A case number looks like this: CAS-01000-HFYET;

The second part 01000 is the sequence number. As far as I know the random suffix is to make sure every number is unique even when cases are created offline and happen to have the same sequence number, i.e. it can happen that two cases are created, one online and one offline that have the same sequence number because the offline client can't check the number. Then the random number still makes it unique.

Question 84: Adding an order lookup in a Case

I am trying to add an Order lookup in the case form so that I can associate a 'Case' when it is initiated by an 'Order'.

How can I do it?

A: Adding an 'Order lookup' to a case form would require you to create a relationship between 'Orders' and 'Cases', and unfortunately you cannot create new relationships in 3.0 that do not involve custom (i.e. user-defined) entities.

Question 85: Relating a case with an account in SDK

I'm trying to create a self-service web form, where customers can enter their unique customer number and create a case by themselves. I want the case to be created and associated to the customer/account with that customer number (custom field).

I successfully managed to create a query and fetch the correct account based on the user input. I have the account id, but I don't know how to associate it to the case. I want to set the customer field to a specific account.

This is my code:

```
account retrievedAccount =
(account)retrieved.BusinessEntities[0];
Guid retrievedAccountGuid =
retrievedAccount.accountid.Value;

incident myIncident = new incident();
myIncident.title = "test";
myIncident.customerid = retrievedAccountGuid;
Guid temp = service.Create(myIncident);
```

Apparently, it's not possible to set the customer field value to an account GUID.

What's the correct way to do this?

A: The customerid is a customer object, so you need to instantiate it first:

```
myIncident.customerid = new Customer();
```

Then set the referenced type and the id:

```
myIncident.customerid.type =
EntityName.account.ToString();
myIncident.customerid.Value = retrievedAccountGuid;
```

Question 86: Deleted Outlook Contacts can't be synchronized

I made the mistake of deleting my Outlook (2003) contacts thinking that CRM would resynchronize but no such luck. Now CRM is ignoring the contacts after I restored them from the 'Deleted Items' folder. There must be a configuration file somewhere that defines contact records downloaded.

Is it possible to force CRM to resynchronize all 'Contacts'?

Is there an XML file somewhere I can delete, perhaps "Contacts.xml"?

A: If something is no longer being synched to Outlook, you may remove any reference to it from the tracking table. You can do the following:

1. Turn off synching for the relevant entity (or change up the data group).
2. Force the Outlook sync.
3. Turn synching back on for the entity.
4. Sync again.
5. Vow to be more careful with deleting in the future.

Question 87: Synchronization

Am I correct in saying, that when you synch an offline, client is the sync date seen as the changed date?

Scenario:

User1 changes record yesterday (offline client) changes phone and fax.

User2 changes the same record today (online client) changes phone.

User1 synch this afternoon, but whose changes are kept? I would assume that whoever last updated the record would have those changes kept. In which case, would be User2.

A: In this case, User 2's change would be lost. The replay that occurs when you go online is just like going in and entering those changes again at that time on the server. But, this is done at the field level so the only time a true conflict occurs is if the 2 users change the same field.

In the situation you outlined, if User 2 had made the phone number change prior to User 1 going offline, User 1 would still have probably changed the phone number to the value he/she wanted it to be.

Question 88: Selected items for synchronization

Is there a way to avoid for a specific appointment not to synchronize with the Outlook calendar, without stopping synchronization with all the other appointments?

A: No. There is no such option as to select only a few items for synchronization.

Question 89: Synchronization Problem

I created a couple of customs' entities. When I turn offline, my custom entities are there but not the data.

What is the best way to synchronize the data of my customs' entities?

A: You should set up two things in customization to successfully do it.

1. The new entity would be available offline in outlook.
2. The entity ownership must be user-owned. Organization isn't good for customization.

Question 90: Error on the Quick Campaign

I have created a Quick Campaign for a great number of leads, with a phone call activity for every lead. I have finished with the steps, and concluded the Quick Campaign, but the activities were not created.

What did I do wrong?

A: It sometimes may take a few minutes to create; depending on the number you have selected to create. The more being created, the longer it might be. When you open the entity page of the Quick Campaign you have created, the Sub Grid display under "phone Calls created" should show the phone call activities. If you do not see them there, please go to "accounts Excluded" in the Quick campaign entity page. Are the leads you selected found here? If so, then the leads you selected for the Quick Campaign may have "Do not send marketing materials" set or "Do not phone" set.

If you are looking elsewhere for your created Activities, such as Workplace Activities, make sure when you create the Quick Campaign that the activities are being assigned to Your account, if not, you may need to change your system view (a combo box found on upper right hand corner of the grid when viewing the MyWork-> Workplace->Activities grid). Change this view from "My Activities" to "All Activities". Your activities are probably being created; you just may need to change the view in order to see them.

Question 91: Sharing leads with non-MS CRMusers

I have a requirement to share leads with distributors who need to receive these leads. They cannot be asked to go to a portal and pull them down.

Is there another way?

A: The simplest way to accomplish this is to export the leads to Excel, and email them. If you need to do this much more frequently, you can consider writing a workflow that could send an email automatically.

Question 92: Follow Up Checks on Leads

I am required to send an email if a lead is not followed up for 24 hours. I tried to create a workflow but got stuck. I tried to create a call assembly which sends email to senior managers but was unsuccessful. I tried to create it through "email", but was unsuccessful due to invalid examples.

How can I create an alert if any activity has been created for the lead in workflow?

Can you guide me here?

A: Workflow is the right way to do this job. You don't need to use workflow assemblies unless you want more flexibility. Let me give an idea how you can achieve this in workflows.

Create a new workflow rule of 'Create' for Lead. It should look like following:

```
/////////////////////////////////////////////////
When lead is created
Wait for 24 hour(s) after Lead.Created On
if
Check any activities created for this entity
then
stop
end if
Email: No activity on Lead : {!Lead Topic;}
/////////////////////////////////////////////////
```

Question 93: Qualify a Lead in JavaScript

I have to perform a number of functions on an ISV button press. One of these is to qualify the 'Lead' and close it without going through the "Convert Lead" button press. For specific reasons, the Lead will not be created as an Account or a Contact, but exported to another program. The "Convert Lead" button will therefore prevent Qualifying a Lead and only allow to Disqualify. I will therefore need to write some JavaScript code to qualify that Lead after I send it to the external application. I know about SetStateLead, but this must be done offline so I only have access to JavaScript.

My code states:

```
// now convert the Lead to Qualified
crmForm.all.statuscode.DataValue = 3; // doesn't seem
to work!
crmForm.Save();
```

How can I do this in JavaScript?

A: There is no way to do this with JavaScript. You could try writing a post callout event that fires when the lead is updated. You could check the value in a picklist to determine if the process that exports the lead to the external process should be fired off. You may remove the convert/disqualify lead from the lead form as well.

Server, Links, Environment, And Web Issues

Question 94: Install on Citrix

I'm looking at installing on a Citrix Xpe environment running on Windows Terminal Server 2003. I see that there is a package in downloads which has a script called "terminstall.cmd". The suggestion is to put the correct parameters in this script and update the user profile to run it on logon.

If it is a small site, would it be ok to run the script manually with the 'install' parameter after logging on as the user?

A: Yes, that would be ok. Just make sure the user already has their Outlook profile configured.

Question 95: Two companies on SBS

Is it possible to implement CRM for two different companies on a Small Business Server?

A: The following should be considered:

1. Are both companies sharing the same Active Directory? Natively, not just using things like email, are their computers authenticating to the domain?

2. You could use the SAME instance of CRM, and create Business Units. If they want drastically different views, however, that could be difficult to set up for them.

3. If you want two separate instances of CRM, then you need an additional web or application server for the 2nd company. I believe that the second company could not use the SBE version of CRM either. They both can use the same SQL server, just can't have more than one CRM web or application server instance on the same physical machine.

Alternatively, if you use the same footprint, it creates problems because CRM v3.0 is not designed for more than one company per box. At the 2006 Convergence there were changes made to the ISP version of MS CRM so one solution might be to use a hosted version of CRM for one company... There are a handful of licensed CRM ISP hosting companies.

Question 96: Creating an incident on the internet

I am using /service/serviceportal.aspx. When I open a new case in http://localhost:1917/service/serviceportal.aspx, it creates the "incident" normally, but when I open a new case in http://danubecrm:1917/service/serviceportal.aspx, operation failed due to a SQL integrity violation.

Platform
System.Web.Services.Protocols.SoapException: Server was unable to process request

at
System.Web.Services.Protocols.SoapHttpClientProtocol.ReadResponse (SoapClientMessage message, WebResponse response, Stream responseStream, Boolean asyncCall)

at
System.Web.Services.Protocols.SoapHttpClientProtocol.Invoke(String methodName, Object[] parameters)

at
danubecrm.CrmService.Create(BusinessEntity entity) in c:\WINDOWS\Microsoft.NET\Framework\v2.0.50727\Temporary ASP.NET

Files\service\01cb73af\d6c7084a\App_WebReferences.i6kadgju.0.cs:line 176

at serviceportal.ImageButton4_Click(Object sender, ImageClickEventArgs e)

in
c:\Inetpub\Development\docs\serviceportal.aspx.cs:line 667

When I create an account or contact in http://localhost:1917/service/serviceportal.aspx, it creates the "account/contact" normally and it works in http://danubecrm:1917/service/serviceportal.aspx.

Why is there a problem when creating my incident on internet, but no problem in local host?

A: This error could have something to do with the way .NET impersonates users. The application will behave differently depending on which URL the user starts the application.

To point you somewhere in the right direction, I see in your code is a danubecrm.CrmService.Create function call. Try setting credentials manually for the call to the CrmService webservice.

```
CrmService service = new CrmService();
service.Credentials = new
NetworkCredential("PrivUserName","PrivUserPassword","
PrivUserDomain");

instead of
service.Credentials =
System.Net.CredentialCache.DefaultCredentials;
```

Question 97: Accessing CRM internally

When I am physically on the CRM server, I can open my IE browser and type in the server name or IP and successfully log into the CRM.

If I am not physically on the CRM server, at a user workstation for example and I type in the server name or IP, it'll prompt me to log in, which I do, but then the browser just closes on me. I do see this though:

"Attempting to open Microsoft CRM. If the application does not load within a few seconds, click here"

If you are asked "if you want to close the current open window, click yes."

Ok, I click yes and my browser closes. If I click no, the browser stays open and I see that message above.

I have three (3) users who get the same thing and can't access the CRM server to do some work.

Why is this happening?

A: A popup blocker is more than likely the cause. That's the behavior you would generally see if you have one or more enabled.

Question 98: Creating test environment

I am trying to redeploy the production CRM into a test environment. Ideally, I do not want to have to create the production users in the test AD.

Is there a way around this?

A: No. There is no way around it. Each user in the production CRM needs to be mapped to a corresponding user in the test deployment. You will have to create the same number of accounts in the test domain, and then map them during the redeployment process. It's a bit tedious, but once the users are created in AD once, your next redeployment will be less painful.

Question 99: Free CRM Server license for Dynamics GP customers

My partner said at a recent user group meeting that MS was offering a free CRM Server license for Dynamics GP customers who are current on their enhancement plan. I'd like to set up and explore using CRM in a small environment (maybe just a few users) and this would make it easier to do.

Unfortunately, my partner isn't being much help on this one, they told me to look on Customer Source, but I can't find anything resembling this.

Do you know where I can go for more details about this program?

A: From December 4th, 2005 onwards, one CRM server license is provided at no additional cost when a customer acquires at least one license of MS Dynamics Professional User. To be eligible, the customer must be either:

1. A current MS Dynamics AX / GP / NAV / SL customer with a current Enhancement Plan from a Business Ready Licensing (Advanced Management Edition only) or Modular Based Licensing (Professional Edition only).

2. A customer purchasing new licenses of MS Dynamics AX / GP / NAV / SL from Business Ready Licensing (Advanced Management Edition only) portion of the Dynamics Price list.

Question 100: Installing Outlook client

Can I install Outlook client in the domain controller, exchange server, and CRM server machines?

In the entity Activity Pointer, which field of state code or status code indicates the state of the activity?

Which value of the status/state code indicates the state achieved 1/0/?

A: The Outlook client is installed on local machines only.

```
StateCode = Status (Open/Close/Canceled).
StatusCode = Status Reason (other items that further
clarify the StateCode).
StateCode of 0 = Open, 1 Closed, 2 Canceled.
```

Please check the StringMap table, it'll tell you all the string values for Int values.

Question 101: Tracking Sent Outlook Mail

I have installed the CRM Outlook Client for 3.0 on a mailbox. I need to track all mail for this mailbox, sent, received, etc. I have selected the option to Track All Messages, but items being sent are not being tracked. This specific mailbox sends automated messages out of it. So we are not physically clicking the new button to construct an email.

Is it possible to get those sent messages to automatically be tracked in CRM?

A: The option 'Track all messages' only applies to incoming emails, not outgoing ones. Outgoing messages will only be tracked if they are generated by CRM, and not otherwise. You say that the messages sent are automated, if they are sent via a CRM mechanism (e.g. workflow), they should be in CRM. But if they are sent by a non-CRM mechanism, they won't be tracked at all. Unless, of course, you choose to (a) change the sending mechanism so that CRM sends them, or possibly (b) cc sent messages into CRM. Of course option (b) will require quite a lot more thought to see if it fits your needs.

Question 102: Moving production CRM database to test environment

I am pretty new to MS CRM but I have to copy our production database to a test environment. I have created a VM, which consists of a DC, MSSQL and Exchange. My test environment is in no way connected to our production environment.

Is there a way on how to do this?

A: You can use the redeployment tools assuming your test environment has its own AD.

Question 103: CRM 3 on Virtual Server

I would like to run CRM on a virtual server.

Will that cause more problems than it's worth?

Is CRM supported running in a virtual environment?

A: According to the CRM3.0 Implementation Guide, Section 5-4:

"Installing Microsoft CRM on a Microsoft Virtual Machine, you can install Microsoft CRM on computers that are running either Microsoft Virtual Server 2005 or Microsoft Virtual PC 2004".

However, note the following support conditions:

1. Because of decreased performance do not use Microsoft CRM running on a virtual machine as your main production business environment.
2. Microsoft CRM Support Services will consider Collaboration Requests and hotfix investigations for issues that involve Microsoft CRM and Microsoft Virtual Server 2005 or Microsoft Virtual PC 2004 only in test, development, and demonstration systems.

Question 104: SDK error while calling webservice from another computer

I created a sample application which creates a new account in MS CRM through SDK. The asp.net application runs fine and inserts new account on the machine in which MSCRM3.0 is installed. Now if I run that application from my machine which is in same domain then it gives me the following error:

"The request failed with HTTP status 401: Unauthorized."

For update function it gives following error:

"Server was unable to process request.

Exception Details:
System.Web.Services.Protocols.SoapException: Server was unable to process request.

Source Error:

Line 351:
[System.Web.Services.Protocols.SoapDocumentMethodAttribute
("http://schemas.microsoft.com/crm/2006/WebServices/Updat
e",
Use=System.Web.Services.Description.SoapBindingUse.Literal,
ParameterStyle=System.Web.Services.Protocols.SoapParameter
Style.Bare)]
Line 352: public void
Update([System.Xml.Serialization.XmlElementAttribute(Names
pace="http://schemas.microsoft.com/crm/2006/WebServices")
] BusinessEntity entity) {
Line 353: this.Invoke("Update", new object[] {
Line 354: entity});
Line 355: }"

I used the following code:

```
CrmService service = new CrmService();
service.Url =
"http://01hw084810:5555/MSCRMServices/2006/CrmService
.asmx";
```

```
service.Credentials =
System.Net.CredentialCache.DefaultCredentials;

// Create an account entity and assign data to some
attributes.
account newAccount = new account();

newAccount.name = "test Greg Bike Store0";
newAccount.accountnumber = "1323456";
newAccount.address1_postalcode = "982052";
newAccount.address1_city = "Redmond";

// Call the Create method to create an account.
Guid accountId = service.Create(newAccount);
```

Where did I go wrong?

A: The main problem is that an ASP application runs under a different context then a normal user. In order to authenticate to CRM, it needs to be able to pass the authentication through the other machine that is often restricted by domain security.

Question 105: Redeploy CRM in environment test

I want to redeploy my CRM in environment test. I don't know if there is no risk to do it.

Is it possible to redeploy it in an OU that is under the OU where I installed my old CRM?

A: I prefer to use a different parent OU just to keep things "clean". The install can create new groups for you. But it can be confusing to see groups with similar names in the same OU.

Question 106: New Server Domain/Same User Domain

My user domain is current and working. However, we want to move the CRM Server to a different domain. It appears that a 'recovery' to a new server in the new domain will work fine. There is no translation of users required.

Current CRM Configuration:
- Users are in DomainA
- Server is in DomainB

Future CRM Configuration:
- Users are in DomainA
- Server is in DomainB

Do I need to follow the 'Redeployment Tool' process or a 'Recovery process'?

A: Yes, I believe that you need to use the redeployment tool.

1. Restore database
2. Run redeployment tool
3. Install CRM against Database

Question 107: Tracking e-mails sent by OWA

When we have set e-mail tracking to 'automatic', and a CRM user sent email from Outlook Web Access, will these emails be tracked under the CRM contact when the email address is recognized?

A: No, they won't. They are 'pure' Exchange messages and CRM doesn't know about them. However, if your users sometimes use Outlook as well as OWA, in Outlook they can open the messages in the sent items and choose to track them in CRM.

Question 108: Install CRM on Exchange server

Are there any issues that I should be aware of when installing CRM 3 on an Exchange server?

Can I install it on an Exchange server?

A: Yes, you can do this, but it is not a recommended approach. If you have a separate Exchange server, you might not want something else on there competing for resources. But it is a supported configuration provided it's not also a DC.

Question 109: ReportServer/Report Access Error in split CRM Architecture

I have Installed CRM and SQL/Reports Server components onto two Windows 2003 Server platforms. The trusted delegations required for Double hop Kerberos authentication and SPN's have been set. The issue is I can run reports from the 'Report Server' within IIS but not from 'Reports' or within the CRM Web or Outlook Clients. When I try to do the function, I get the following error:

"An error has occurred during report processing. (rsProcessingAborted). Cannot create a connection to data source 'Microsoft_CRM_MSCRM'. (rsErrorOpeningConnection). Login failed for user '(null)'. Reason: Not associated with a trusted SQL Server connection. "

What is confusing is that both the 'Reports Server' and 'Reports directories' are using the same ODBC connector.

How do I solve this?

A: In my instance I could run reports from the server, logged on as the crmadmin, but couldn't from any other client machines.

Following the advice of MS, I logged onto the report server interface and modified the permissions of the Microsoft CRM Connector to remove integrated security and fix the connection to run under the user name that I found worked.

This raised questions about the integrity of the data returned. Now I was running reports under the crmadmin account, but have been assured that it will still use the security applied by the CRM security role of the user running the report and not just return data based on crmadmin's system administrator role.

1. Open Report Manager (on the SRS server, go to http://localhost/reports).
2. Click the Show Details button.
3. Click on the <orgname_MSCRM> folder.

4. Find MSCRM DataSource among the list of reports and click it.
5. In the "Connect Using" section, note that the default is "Windows NT Integrated Security".
6. Change it to "Credentials stored securely in the report server".
7. Enter a username and password of an admin user.
8. Mark the checkboxes for "Use as Windows credentials..." and "Impersonate the authenticated user..."
9. Apply the changes and test 'Reports'.

Question 110: Two CRM implementations on same server

Is it possible to have two (2) different CRM implementations and installations on the same CRM server?

Is it possible to switch Outlook clients during application launch in between two (2) different CRM implementations?

A: You need one web server per deployment; however, both SQL databases can be on the same SQL server. You cannot have outlook switch between deployments. You would have to uninstall/reinstall the SFO client.

Question 111: Change of path in Outlook to CRM 3.0 server

I have a message from Outlook: "There is a problem communicating with CRM Server, etc."

Where can I change the path in Outlook to CRM 3.0 server?

A: You can change it from the registry. The directory below can guide you.

HKEY_CURRENT_USER\Software\Microsoft\MSCRMClient

Question 112: Homepage from 1.2 available somewhere

Is the homepage from 1.2 available somewhere or do we have to create one that looks like it used to?

I believe I would use Sharepoint to create one.

A: Your best option would be to do the following:

1. Create some CRM web parts.
2. Bring those into a Sharepoint Site.
3. Add a link to your sitemap which points to that Sharepoint Site and then you could be set.

Question 113: Moving databases to new server

We are running CRM3 in the usual three (3) server configuration running CRM, SQL 2000, and Exchange 2003.

I have a shiny new server with SQL 2005 on it and I'd like to move the CRM databases and reporting services onto it.

Is it as simple as detaching and copying the databases?

A: There will be a few additional steps.

1. CRM will need to be hanged to "point" to the other DB. This can be done via Deployment Manager.
2. You will need to manually create the SQL logins for all the associated SQL users & AD groups. Without this step, there will be problems with SQL security. You may also run into some issues with this step if you are using local system accounts for access.

Question 114: Development Installation of CRM 3.0

We have CRM 3.0 running on our domain.

Can I install CRM 3.0 on a machine in our domain that will be used for development and not run into issues with the production machine?

A: This will work although I have seen an issue once when two CRM deployments were somehow cross linked. Keep the development system on a single server with web and SQL and you should be fine.

Another option would be to add a new forest and domain which runs on your network. This can be used for development work.

Lastly consider using virtual PC for development work. I don't know how many developers you are working with but it's a good option.

Question 115: Deployment of CRM Server

Is it possible to deploy Dynamics CRM 3.0 as a one-box deployment with a DC controller running on the same machine?

A: Yes it is possible. That's exactly the scenario covered by the CRM3.0 Small Business Edition. But it's only supported on Windows Small Business Server 2003.

Question 116: Import v1.2 customizations into 3.0

I have exported my CRM 1.2 customizations to an XML file. I tried and get the error message: "This is not a valid customization file".

How do I import them to 3.0 on another server?

A: You cannot take 1.2 customizations and import to version 3.0. You would need to upgrade the 1.2 server to 3.0. Then you could move customizations from that server to the other one.

Question 117: SBS CRM 3.0 or SQL 2000 or SQL2005

After reading a ton of issues with SQL 2005 report services, I have a blank canvas and am left wondering what the best approach is to use after installing SBS 2003. Should I install and stay with SQL 2000 or SQL 2005?

A: Assuming you are using the CRM SBE and SBS 2003 (pre-R2) then you'd best stay with SQL 2000. SQL 2005 won't be part of SBS until SBS R2 is released. So from a licensing point of view, you really don't have a choice.

I have SBS R2 installed on a VPC and intend to do a test install of CRM SBE. However, I'm not sure what exactly I will be able to report as the EULA for the R2 beta has a confidentiality clause in it.

Question 118: Active Directory

Is it safe to install CRM3 on company's production 'Active Directory'?

A: Yes, it's safe to do so. CRM does not change the AD schema. It does however require that an OU and a few security groups be created. I would instead recommend you to setup a test environment perhaps using virtual PC so you can get a feel for how CRM works, etc.

Question 119: Upgrade CRM 3.0 Beta to CRM3.0 RTM

We have one terrible problem.

When CRM 3.0 beta came out, we didn't understand that Microsoft is not going to support upgrading it to a final version, so we upgraded our CRM 1.2 to CRM 3.0 Beta. Now when we try to upgrade CRM 3.0 Beta to CRM 3.0 RTM installer says that the database is not supported.

More details about environment & what we tried to do is Server - Windows 2003, SQL 2000, and Exchange 2003 with the latest packs. We had CRM 1.2 installed and then upgraded it to CRM 3.0 Beta.

Now, if I try to Uninstall CRM 3.0 Beta, and then try to install CRM 3.0 RTM it says "Database not supported". We've got a lot of information there and cannot afford to lose it.

I need to know if I should change the database to make it compatible to 3.0 RTM or if maybe there could be some tools to do this.

Will it be possible to extract all the data from current database and then import it back to RTM Database?

A: The Beta agreement made it clear that this upgrade would NOT be supported. The biggest issue you face is that the Beta code could have introduced a corruption in the database due to a code glitch.

I would try contacting Scribe (www.scribesoft.com) as their tool may be able to help you. The other option is to build code via the SDK that pulls from the beta version of the DB and inserts to the prod DB via the API's.

There are companies that can help you with this. They have utilities in-house which would enable them to help you get your data out of Beta 3.0 and into RTM 3.0.

If this is of interest please call the following no. +44(0) 1635 570970, or contact them through their website at www.mscrm-cabc.co.uk.

Question 120: Loading CRM V1.2 for demo

I am trying to load up CRM V1.2 just to have demo copy to play with, etc. I set up a server Windows 2003 with latest SP, SQL 2000 w/ SP3, IIS, and am now trying to load the Exchange Server and from there, load the CRM V1.2 software.

Can I load this all on one blank server used for nothing but this purpose?

I am having trouble with the Exchange 2003 load because it states that I need to have the NNTP service running. However, I can't find this in the components list so I can begin running it.

What else do I need to load?

A: Yes, you can run all of these on a single server, though it is not a supported configuration. I run my demo environments like this via a Virtual PC.

The NNTP service may need to be added via Windows setup by selecting it in the Windows Components.

Question 121: Email Template View

When attempting to create a case email and selecting the "insert template" link, only four (4) template choices are available, and none of which apply to "Case".

What is the procedure to make all template selections available at that screen?

A: After clicking the "Insert Template", another window pops up where you should select either the Recipient or the 'Regarding' object. You should select the 'Regarding' object (the case) otherwise you see the templates based on the 'Recipient' object type.

Question 122: MS CRM 3.0 over the internet

Can I access MS CRM over the internet?

A: We are experimenting this and it works great.

1. Forward the port 5555 into your router to the internal server IP.
2. Go to IE into your outside pc add, the address of your forwarded DNS is like (http://crm.domain.com:5555) to trusted site and it works.

But OU is not really secure because if anybody knows log & pass, they can access your CRM from everywhere.

Question 123: IE log in error

I've just installed Microsoft CRM on a test server and imported the sample database. From the server, I can log in fine with both administrator and the 5 sample users when using IE. When I try to log in from a remote client, IE just closes even though it seems that the login is fine. If I write a wrong username or password, I get an error telling me that one or the other isn't valid. The client is running XP home as the operating system, and the CRM-system is running on a SBS 2K3.

Why does the browser simply get shot down?

A: Most likely the problem is, the remote client has a popup blocker. When CRM starts, the initial page opens a new window, and then closes itself.

Question 124: Upgrade Windows 2003 server

I run the CRM web on one server and the SQL on another one, neither one is currently SP1.

Is it recommended to upgrade my Windows 2003 server to SP1 yet?

What about the SQL 2000 SP4 update?

A: I am not sure what others have to say but we upgraded our environment because of important security updates to the OS. Besides, Microsoft has the CRM update for XP sp2 and Win2k3 Server SP1. See the Rollup for CRM1.2. It has all the updates since the 1.2 release. Also, lookout for some manual updates to IE on the desktops.

Question 125: Effect of e-mail router on default web site

I'm looking at the Implementation Guide for CRM version 1.2. On page 192 where it explains how to install the Email Router, it says this:

"11. On the Select Installation Locations page, accept the Default Web Site and file installation directory, and then click 'Next'. On this page, the Default Web Site is the Web site on the computer on which you are installing the Router, not the Microsoft CRM server."

This had me worried. Since I'm installing the Email Router on an Exchange server, I'm concerned about what exactly it is going to do to that default web site. IIS as you know is real critical for Exchange to function.

I'm installing CRM first in our test lab but I'm not even eager to destroy an Exchange server in the lab if I can prevent it.

Can you explain what exactly happens on the Exchange server when I do this install?

A: It will not affect the Exchange server. All it does is add a virtual directory under the website that will house a web service.

Question 126: Multiple CRM Installations

We are looking at hosting a CRM solution for a number of small companies.

Are we able to use a single domain with 1 CRM server, 1 Exchange server and 1 SQL server to house more than 1 CRM instance?

If not are we able to add new SQL and CRM servers for each client to the domain and run it that way?

Or do we need a separate domain for each client?

A: This should be possible. I know some implementations where there would be multiple CRM implementations in the same domain. But they do use different SQL servers. Remember CRM is very SQL intensive, so be careful with the load on the SQL server. You should use different license codes for each company so a 4 different databases will be created in the SQL server and a different OU is created in the Active Directory. This way the data and roles won't interfere.

Question 127: Issues on SBS2003 SP1 on MS CRM 1.2

Are there any problems with the Service Pack 1 for Small Business Server 2003 on a server with Microsoft CRM 1.2?

A: Yes, there is.

After this patch was installed the SFO failed to replicate. I tracked it down to the publishers snapshot failed with the following message:

"The process could not bulk copy out of table 'filt14DBFF2D718747969992058D9437BE48'.

ODBCBCP/Driver version mismatch";

The DLLS sqlsvr32.dll and odbcbcp.dll had different versions. The ODBC have not been updated by the MDAC 2.8 sp1 which was deployed with SBS SP1. It logged a case with MS support that sent the updated DLLS – with the entire same version. SFO now replicates.

Question 128: Error in installing Action Pack of MS CRM1.2

I am trying to install our Action Pack copy of MS CRM 1.2 onto our server running SBS 2003 & having chosen to install CRM, we see an error message. Clicking 'OK' returns us to the desktop.

What can I do to rectify this?

A: You can do the following steps:

1. Go to Administrative Tools>Services>.
2. Locate the 'Indexing Service' and set it to 'Automatic' and then start it.
3. Restart the installation of CRM.

Question 129: SFO User problem

After I've installed SFO on Outlook 2003, it works fine as long as I log on to this computer. The problem I have starts after another user logs on to the same computer with his account. It seems that SFO doesn't exist for this user. A reinstall under this second user gives a popup that it is already installed. But uninstalling gives an error that it is only possible for installed components.

Second problem I have is that the default service on MSDE does not start automatically. I am working in a testing environment so I can play as much as I want.

How can I solve this?

A: Sales for Outlook only supports one user per machine. So only one user can login to a machine, launch and use Sales for Outlook.

Question 130: Error in MS CRM setup

Every time I try to install Microsoft CRM, I get this error
message:

"Setup was unable to install Microsoft CRM Server.
Setup was unable to create the Microsoft CRM databases.
Failed to run script:00 - create mscrm.sql.
HRESULT:80040E14.
Unknown error. (80040E14)".

I get this message after putting in my key, the SQL server to use,
and what active directory location to install it under. Right when
the progress bar shows to start the installation, it shows this
message and terminates.

This is on a Windows 2003 Small Business Server Premium
Edition.

I've also tried reinstalling SP3a for SQL Server.

What is the cause of this error message?

A: This error is caused by one of two things:

1. When you have multiple domain controllers that aren't
    replicating fast enough; however, in your case that's not the
    problem as you are running a Small Business Server.

2. It is possible you have the CRM SQL database files still left
    on the system.

Question 131: SQL server error

I'm installing CRM according to the getting started guide. When I want to select the server that runs SBS 2003 when the wizards asks for the server where SQL server is running I don't find the main computer name of the server to choose from ('SERVER') but I do find SERVER\BKUPEXEC, likely relating it to the backup program named 'Veritas Backup Exec' that is installed.

Looking under services I find SQLAgent$BKUPEXEC and SQLAgent$SBSMONITORING active and running but no other plain SQL Server service. 'Backup Exec' runs fine on that SQL server.

When I select SERVER\BKUPEXEC during CRM setup it comes however with a message 'function for full text indexes should be active on that server'.

What does that phrase mean - how to tackle?

Should I proceed this way or should I somehow reinstall SQL server? How?

A: One way to see if the full version of Microsoft SQL Server has been installed is to go to the 'Add/Remove Programs' on your SBS server. Microsoft SQL Server should be listed there. Another place to check is under Start > Programs, you should see Microsoft SQL Server listed and then sub components such as Enterprise Manager, Query Analyzer, etc. It sounds like SQL is not installed on this server. The reason I say that is, because earlier you stated that you are only seeing 2 services relating to your backup software. The SQLAgent$ services probably are MSDE instances of some sort that possibly get installed, but it sure doesn't sound like the full versions are there. You may double-check those things.

Question 132: Installing CRM in SBS 2003 Premium environment

We have the SBS premium with 20 users with Great Plains installed, and a terminal server 2003. I also have 2-2000 servers P-III/600 dual processors that are sitting idle. I am looking to utilize the 2 idle servers to implement CRM. When I was reading the documentation, it recommends installing separate SQL server. There is also a separate SMTP server for CRM. There was a mention on installing CRM on TS; Our TS is not being used to its potential, it is a P4 Dual Xeon with RAID.

What do you recommend?

A: You have to remember that even though your old servers are dual PIII's, etc. they are still slow CPU's at 600 MHz. They will work but your users may complain of slow performance. At best, you should use them as the CRM web server and use a faster server for the database. The CRM outlook client is installed on each user's computer; you cannot use it in a terminal server environment.

Question 133: MSCRM3.0 & Active Directory

I am having a problem in finding an active directory group for MSCRM. I need help on how MSCRM3.0 create groups in active directory and what are those groups. I am trying to set up a document library at Sharepoint and I don't want to add each of my MSCRM users individually. In Sharepoint document library, I can add domain groups. In this way I simply add domain groups in Sharepoint rather than add individual users.

How does MSCRM handle users in Active directory and domain groups?

A: There are several ways to get to the groups, but here's what I usually do:

Open SQL Server Management Studio (or Enterprise Manager) and navigate to the CRM database. Expand the tree and select the security node.

You will see two groups, named like this:

DOMAIN\ReportingGroup {Some Guid here}
DOMAIN\SQLAccessGroup {Same Guid as above}

The ReportingGroup should contain all CRM users. But to double-check, open AD Users and Computers, search for this group and display the group members.

Question 134: Security warning in Outlook client

I have developed a custom ASP.NET Web Service. I call a function from this service when the user clicks on a new button in the quote form. This works both on the server and on a client machine using the web interface. However, when I click on the button in the Outlook client online, I get a security warning: "This page is accessing information that is not under its control. This poses a security risk. Do you want to continue?" When I press "Yes" the function executes without a problem.

How do I solve this?

A: You may do the following work: In IE open Internet Options and switch to the security tab. Select Local Intranet and hit the "Custom Level" button. There is an option named 'Access Data Sources across Domains' which should be set to "Prompt". Setting it to "Enable" may solve your issue. I'm assuming that your problem is related to this as you're accessing a service in a different domain.

Question 135: Add or remove link under My Work

How can I add or remove link as "Calendar, Account, Report ....."
under 'My Work' in the main CRM?

A: This is controlled via the Sitemap. To modify this, refer to
the SDK as it explains the format of the file. You first need to
export this from the customizations, edit it, then import it back
in. Make sure to retain the original file though.

Question 136: Checking Online Status

I've got a demo system setup and have made a few changes to
showcase CRM. One of the things I have done is tied the
'Contact' form into a simple website that locates the contact's
website login and displays it. This works fine. What I want to be
able to do is hide this IFrame when the CRM Client is in offline
mode since a connection to the website is no longer guaranteed.

Is there a way to programmatically check on form load if the
CRM Client is operating in online or offline mode?

A: Yes, the method is named 'IsOnline'. The SDK
documentation contains it in the topic "Global."

Question 137: Creating a pilot installation on a CRM server

I want to create a pilot installation on a customer's test CRM server using the customer's pre-existing AD structure which needs reorganization. I am unsure if taking the defaults during the CRM installation will be a good idea being fairly new to real world implementations, so would like some advice on the best way forward to avoid any potential pitfalls.

I have successfully performed an Adventure Works Cycle test installation on another system successfully, so I think I understand most of the issues, but have realized I may not be 100% sure of the relationship between AD and CRM, as I have read the implementation guide and the CRM/AD FAQ, and am still not completely sure of the best way to proceed.

The customer's AD structure is currently organized geographically, within their internal DNS domain name e.g. a.b.org.

A.
- Domain Controllers

B.
- Company
- UK
- London

The pilot will initially only be used by the IT department, and all of these users are currently in the "London" OU, with various security groups applied.

When installing CRM, it defaults the organizational unit to b, and the organization name as "Company" from the license. I am unsure if this will cause a problem as an OU for the Company already exists in AD, or will it cope with this and create something like a\b\Company\Company (in a similar manner to tld.org\Adventure Works Cycle\Adventure Works Cycle)?

The customer's AD will be reorganized in the future, so I guess it might be a good idea to keep the CRM OU separate in order to avoid conflicts.

I presume if I take the defaults, the CRM OUs corresponding to each Business Unit will be created under the lowest "Company" OU, so there shouldn't be a conflict with the pre-existing OUs under the higher level "Company OU".

Is this correct? And if so, is it normal that CRM business units are created independently of the main AD hierarchy, or can CRM use existing AD OUs (and is this recommended)?

A: If users will be spread out then a geographically based OU for CRM may not work. However, you might want to consider creating an application level OU and store CRM under that.

Other Issues

Question 138: Report handling by CRM

If I use the SQL Reporting Engine for Reports, how does CRM handle the 'Reports' and in which Format, RDL or RDLC?

A: According to the Microsoft CRM 3.0 SDK, you will use .rdl files to upload reports. Please refer to the topic "Report Writers Guide" in the SDK.

Question 139: "multi-user client" and "single-user-client"

I am a sales person and prepare a presentation in CRM 3.0 for a customer. I have problems understanding the outlook client user-rights.

In desktop outlook client, what does the multi-user client-capability means?

Does this means, I have a desktop client for outlook, and many users can open an instance of this client with different logins?

For laptop client means single-user client that allows only one instance of this client.

A: Sometimes several users share a single PC. This means users can login to the PC using a unique username/password. Next they can start Outlook, and use the Microsoft CRM Outlook (desktop) client. The desktop makes it possible that every user can login to the PC and use the Microsoft CRM for Outlook client.

However, for laptops the scenario is a little bit different. Laptops are, most of the time, used by a single user. This user will probably be on the move, so offline capability is needed. For this, the laptop client includes a lightweight version of SQLServer, SQLServer 2005 express edition. To be able to synchronize data, a far more complex architecture is used. However, this will currently not allow facilitating more than one user. So trying to install the laptop client for more than one user will not work. In fact the installation program will prevent you from doing so.

Question 140: User Print Option

I have a user that has a customized security role, but the user can't find the print option.

Which option should I enable in his security role?

A: You can do this:

Settings -> Business Unit Settings -> Security Roles -> <<Custom
Security Role>> -> Business Management -> Miscellaneous
Privileges -> Print - provide full access here;

Question 141: Creating ticket with sent email

Is it possible that when you create a ticket, you have it automatically send an email with the client's details and ticket number for reference?

A: Yes, it is very much possible. You may use workflow for this purpose.

Workflow allows you to send email activities after some condition. Even if your particular requirement is not met with workflow, you may develop some workflow assembly to achieve your exact desired requirement.

Question 142: Limit search results by view

Is it possible to limit the scope of the search function to just retrieve values from the list that is filtered by the filtered view that is selected in the views combo box?

For example: In the 'Activities' list, if I select the "closed tasks" view, and then run a simple search, I just want to get results regarding closed tasks.

A: Yes, it is possible. This is a by-design behavior.

When you use the search box, you use a different view, the "quick find" view; which uses a different fetch xml than the view you select on the right; thus the search results are on a different set - usually a complete set.

If you want to further filter the selected view, you can use the alphanumeric filter on the bottom; those ones are applied on top of the selected view's filter.

If you really want this functionality I see two possibilities:

1. Edit the quick find view fetch xml to restrict the search scope but this is rather specific and dangerous as it will restrict all searches for that entity.
2. Add a button or menu linking to a custom made .aspx pop-up page which can asks for the search criteria and further filter the records.

Question 143: Price List Decimals

How can I change the price list decimal to .001?

A: An option you could use is in Settings/Settings/Organization Settings/ System Settings/General/"Pricing Decimal Precision".

Question 144: Direct email without history entry

I would like to send Direct emails to a large number of contacts (>10,000) in our CRM system. I don't want to save this email in contact history. It would be a waste of space saving the emails in history every time I send direct emails.

How do I block CRM from making the History entry for direct emails?

A: You cannot block CRM from creating emails, but you can do delete emails automatically after they are sent. You may use callouts for this purpose.

Question 145: Photo display in Contact

Is there a possibility to show a picture on a tab for the contacts so that the picture is automatically shown instead of opening a picture as attachment in notes?

A: There are two possibilities:

1. If you don't need offline functionality, a solution would be to create an .aspx page which displays the photo related to a certain contact guide. The photo itself could be store in the crm notes entity or in an external store. An example would be an existing HR application or an external database. This .aspx page can then be accessed with a contact form tab using an IFRAME object. Be sure to select the check box to get the guide parameter sent to the form.

2. If you do need offline functionality, the notes attachment is the easiest path. You could deploy the solution 1 locally to all clients but it would be quite a pain to maintain and synch.

Question 146: Saving a file with edits

When I export as a Dynamic Excel file and make edits, I save the file, and when I re-open it I lose my edits.

How can I save the file with my edits?

A: You may copy the entire contents of the Excel spreadsheet, open a new one, and do a "paste special" and paste in the values. That will separate the data from the dynamic query that generated it.

Question 147: Create an Opportunity using a workflow

I need to have a workflow check the Contract End Date on an order or an opportunity. If the contract end date is nearing, I would like to create a new opportunity.

CRM allows you to create activities, but not an instance of an entity like 'Opportunity'. The customer would really like to see a new opportunity be created 90 days prior to the contract expiring. They want to be able to forecast for it.

How may I do this?

A: The only way to do this is through code. In this case a workflow assembly would be the best bet, which requires some .Net coding knowledge. The CRM SDK will get you started.

Question 148: isv.config won't stick

I have exported isv.config configuration using the export tool and added a Navigation Bar node under an <Entity> (tried both custom and system) then re-imported the configuration successfully and published, but when viewing the entity in MS CRM, the navigation bar item doesn't appear.

Can you help me?

A: You can enable ISV Integration in your web.config-file. The line could be as follows:

```
<add key="ISVIntegration" value="All" />;
```

Question 149: Change the CRM Port

I have an installation of MS CRM 3.0 that is accessed by the following URL http://crmserver:5555. I need to change the port to 5566 because my backup software works on 5555 port.

Can I change directly the port on CRM web site properties (IIS ADMIN)?

And on Outlook client installation, do I need to reinstall all clients or do I have the possibility to change the port on any configuration file?

A: You can change the port in IIS administration, and then you have to change registry values on the CRM Server and all clients. The server registry values are under HKLM\Software\Microsoft\MSCRM, and the client ones are under HKCU\Software\Microsoft\MSCRMClient. I suppose there are two (2) values to change in each case.

Question 150: CRM automatically track emails

A user has sent an email from with Outlook who has CRM for outlook desktop client to a friend who is not in the CRM system. The CRM has automatically tracked it and attached it to an email campaign.

What is causing it?

A: Any mail that has the 'track in CRM' button toggled will be tracked in CRM. Also, their user setting may be set to track all email. Please see personal options in CRM.

Question 151: Import Active Directory users/roles to CRM

Is there a way to import Active Directory users/roles to Microsoft CRM?

A: CRM 3.0 provides the user setup wizard from the Deployment Manager. It allows you to select multiple entries from your AD and bulk-create their CRM profiles.

Question 152: Showing added services to Kit Products

We sell bundled services and although I can set them up in the CRM, how do the services you add to your kit product show on your opportunity or order?

A: The kit almost acts like any other product record. It won't break into its various components "line item products" automatically via out of box. It does give you the logical tracking of other product "bundle" behind the scene. Not much intelligence beside that.

Some things to consider:

1. Does this integrate with ERP, like Great Plains, the integration does impact this area.
2. If you're using Kit and want to view the break down components or "bundle services" in the order, you will need to look into SDK.
3. There are 3rd Party Quote/Order/"Configurator" solutions that give more options in this area, like Experlogix, http://www.experlogix.com/.

Question 153: Implementing replication with CRM database

I would like to implement replication in CRM database but since the SQL server instance is "LOCAL" by default, it's not allowing me to configure replication.

Is there a way to solve this?

What kind of replication is recommended with CRM database (both metabase and CRM database)?

A: In Enterprise Manager or SQL Server Management Studio delete the SQL Server registration for LOCAL and then add another registration for the server by name.

Question 154: CRM 3.0 Client Installation won't recognize Outlook Version

I get the following error when installing the CRM 3.0 Client.

"Setup failed to determine whether a supported version of Microsoft Outlook is installed...."

I have used Outlook many times so I already did the CRM help suggestion of starting Outlook to set the default user profile.

What can I do to fix this?

A: You can do the following:

- "Under HKCU\Software\Microsoft create a registry entry for MSCRMClient
- Under MSCRMClient create a new reg_dword key called "IgnoreChecks"
- Make the value 1";

Rerun the installation. You will get the same error, however the 'Next' button will be available and the install should complete without errors.

Question 155: Deleting cancelled invoice

A cancelled invoice cannot be deleted. I am getting the message "cannot be deleted because read only". Because of this the opportunity and the contact also cannot be deleted.

How do I delete this?

A: If you are willing to go with an unsupported solution, then you can update the State Code column directly in the SQL Table and set it to 1. You should then be able to delete the record via the UI.

Question 156: End User Training

I am trying to develop a user's guide for my company. We need something with lots of pictures etc.

Do you have any ideas?

A: You can purchase the training guides that Microsoft uses for their training classes. Contact an MBS partner for pricing.

Alternatively, you can build your own using Microsoft word by grabbing screenshots, etc. and adding captions.

Question 157: Reinstall or wipe the database

I've been playing around with the sample database, and now I would like to start using my companies' own data.

Should I do a complete reinstall or can I wipe the database and the Adventure Works Cycle company information?

A: You should not use the Adventure Works Cycle installation for production environments. If you wish to use your personal license, you will have to reinstall CRM by design. Deleting the data from the database directly is not supported.

Question 158: Wrong name registration

We made an implementation and when almost finished, we recognized that we registered the product to a wrong organization name at MBS/Customer Source web pages.

What effects can we expect and do we need to re-do the whole implementation from the beginning?

A: If you are saying that the license key(s) you have are for the wrong Org Name, you can contact MBS and they can change that and re-issue new keys. However, the Org Name doesn't affect anything in the system, so if you don't mind the name, there is no harm in keeping it.

Question 159: Microsoft CRM and McAfee 8.0 problems

I have a general question, when McAfee 8.0 is installed on a client MS CRM (the Web and SFO) doesn't work anymore.

Can you tell me which settings in McAfee 8.0 are required so that MS CRM and McAfee can coexist on the same client?

A: There is a setting with this release of McAfee Enterprise Edition 8.0 that prevents Outlook from launching items from the TEMP directory. When clicking on the MSCRM folders in the SFO Client, the client will produce the '/' Application Error referencing the Machine.Config file. The resolution is listed below.

RESOLUTION:

1. Right Click Virus Scan in the Taskbar
2. Virus Console.
3. Double Click Access Protection
4. Select File, Share, and Folder Protection.
5. Deselect > Prevent Outlook from launching anything from the TEMP folder.

In addition, the Rules at the Server AV may need to be changed so they don't republish the rules to workstations.

Question 160: SFO CRM Folders Display Issue

The CRM folders in SFO won't display. When I select any one of the folders, such as Account, I get the following error message:

"Action canceled
Internet Explorer was unable to link to the Web page you requested. The page might be temporarily unavailable.

Please try the following:

Click the Refresh button, or try again later.

If you have visited this page previously and you want to view what has been stored on your computer, click File, and then click Work Offline.

For information about offline browsing with Internet Explorer, click the Help menu, and then click Contents and Index."

I have tried clearing the forms cache in Outlook and I have re-installed SFO from scratch. The CRM buttons on the toolbar work fine.

How do I solve this?

A: Please check the following information on the workstation experiencing the issues with the Sales for Outlook client.

1. Verify Registry entries for Microsoft CRM are correct:

1. Please click Start | Run | type Regedit.
2. Navigate to the the following registry key:
HKEY_Local_Machine | Software | Microsoft | MSCRM.
3. Verify that ServerUrl key states the actual name of the CRM Server and not the IP address (example: http://crmserver/MSCRMServices).

4. Also make sure the WebAppUrl displays the name of the
    CRM Server and not the IP address (example:
    http://crmserver).

2. Verify Internet Explorer settings:
1. Open an Internet Explorer browser and click Tools | Internet
    Options | Connections | LAN Settings.
2. Uncheck everything, but "Automatically detect settings".
3. Click Ok.

Once done, restart Outlook and then see if the error occurs. If it
does, can you right-click on one of the CRM folders in Outlook
and select properties.

Click the home page tab and copy and paste the address into IE.

Question 161: Conflict tables

We installed the "CRM MSDN" license, and after an installation we saw the following:

The MSDN_Subscriber_MSCRM database contains tables like:

- conflict_CRMPub-MSDN_Subscriber_MSCRM_AccountBase
- conflict_CRMPub-MSDN_Subscriber_MSCRM_AccountLeads
- ....

and the MSDN_Subscriber_METABASE database contains tables like:

- conflict_CRMMetaPub-
MSDN_Subscriber_METABASE_Attribute
- conflict_CRMMetaPub-
MSDN_Subscriber_METABASE_AttributeMap
- ...

What are these tables used for?

A: These tables are completely out of your control. They are used to detect conflicts between replicated databases such as someone modifying the same record and then trying to merge those changes back together. The tables closely mirror the size of the associate CRM table, with a few extra fields added.

The 8000 limit is not a hard limit in SQL in terms of the table def. It's a hard limit in terms of the actual data stored in the table. The table def can go beyond 8000, CRM just won't allow that to happen with its tables. Thus, even though the record size may be slightly larger that the base CRM table, it should not be an issue unless you have maxed out every field on the record.

Question 162: Editable View

I want to create in CRM some sort of view in which I can add checkboxes that can be updated by the user. The functional requirement is that a user has a paper list which should be checked against the CRM customer. All customers who are on that list should be marked in CRM. There are approximately 300 customers on that list and we don't want to jump to the details screen of that customer to mark it.

Is this possible?

A: You cannot include checkboxes in the view. But you can select multiple records at once and use the bulk edit feature to mark more than one record at a time.

Question 163: Business Unit System Administrator

I am having 2 Business Units in CRM, and I want to maintain 2 System Administrator each of BU. System Administrator of one BU should not be able to change any Roles in another BU.

Is it possible?

A: Yes, it is possible in Roles customization form, "Business Management" Tab, Enity "Role". Select "Parent: Child Business Units" instead of "Organization" and same for other entities/tabs.

Question 164: Change of site map

I have changed site map to reorder the navigation elements. It is working fine for web client but I don't know why it is not showing same order in outlook client.

Am I missing something?

A: This is a very expected behavior. Actually, web client do show items according to the order of site map but outlook client shows folders and they are always in alphabetical order and not according to site map order.

Question 165: Blank Spaces in Text Box

I am using logic in which takes string as input. It returns error if there is space in the string. So, I want to check the user input in text box for blank spaces.

How do I do it with Jscript?

A: Depending on what you need, you can use either the String.indexOf method or the String.replace. The first lets you check if there is a space in the string, while the second can be used to replace them. You will find the entire Jscript documentation in the Microsoft Scripting Technologies Site (http://www.microsoft.com/scripting).

A2: You can put this code in "Onchange" of your Text Box:

```
var check=crmForm.all.<fieldname>.DataValue;

var space=check.indexOf(" ");
if(parseInt(space,10)!=-1)
{
alert("White Space is not allowed in code field");
event.returnValue=false;
}
--
```

Question 166: DataGrid paging

I have created a custom page to display data from another database. This page includes a datagrid with paging enabled. When I run the page outside of CRM the page works fine, but when it runs within crm (accessible as a navigation option) the paging does not work. It appears that the pageindexchanged event is not triggered, but the pageload event is executed.

Why would it not work within the crm UI when it works correctly as a stand-alone page?

A: CRM disables viewstate, which is required by a lot of controls. You need to provide an override in the web.config of your virtual app to override this and reenable viewstate.

Question 167: Workflow Parameters

I created a new workflow. When a case is assigned, I send an email to the owner. My problem is my variables are not displayed in my email.

Example: (Hi {!Case:Owner;},) is displayed like that and not Hi Sophie Beaulieu,

Here is my workflow. I don't know why is not working.

```
To:
-------------------------------------------------------
[owner]
Subject:
-------------------------------------------------------
A new Case is assigned to you CaseeNumber:
{!Case:Case Number;} Title:
{!Case:Title;} SystemID: {!Case:System ID;}

Description:
-------------------------------------------------------
Hi {!Case:Owner;},
A new case is Assigned to you: {!Case:Title;} .
Thank you.
Case Information
Case Number: {!Case:Case Number;}
Case Title: {!Case:Title;}
Description: {!Case:Description;Case:Description;}
Customer: {!Case:Customer;}
```

What is wrong?

A: The problem is because you are giving case:owner. You need to use Owner:fullname in your email.

-   Select "send mail"
-   To do this go to Insert Action -> Send mail
-   Go to MS CRM Rule Editor
-   Say "new"
-   Select entity "Owner" (Probably you are missing this step)
-   Select field Full name

Question 168: Hide Quick Campaign from Sales Area

I know we can hide the link in the left hand navigation. For example, to hide the link to Activities you would use navActivities.style.display = "none".

Now, I want to hide the Quick Campaign from Sales Area but I cannot write the script since there is no form load.

How can I do it?

A: You can hide Quick campaign by removing it from the "sales" area in "Sitemap".

Question 169: Removing activities from queue

Is there any way to remove activities from a queue In Progress other than to delete it?

A: Completing the activities will remove them from the In Progress queue.

Question 170: CRM software architecture - External business layer

We're developing our own CRM, which is integrated with other systems and receiving marketing data from external databases. We've got some business logic at forms level, so we can monitor data quality
in the OnLoad and OnSave events easily. But the same business logic has to be executed and validated by some external systems, so we'd like to have an external validations layer, which can be invoked by the external systems and by the CRM. Something like a DLL would be perfect, but we've got two doubts about this solution architecture:

1. Is this feasible? Is the Forms code capable to invoke external functions available in a DLL? Does the DLL have to be distributed among desktop clients or will it be invoked only by the applications server?

2. Is there any better architecture?

A: You may use Microsoft.XmlHttp ActiveX, which is a common thing now in CRM SDK, and IE by default do not block this ActiveX. You can invoke any webservice or any web page that return XML format. This way it will execute through some webserver like the web application in CRM Server itself, so there is no deployment issue at all.

Another way is through CRM Callout.

Question 171: Fire workflow automatically

I am trying to send an email on contacts' birthdays. I have done it when applying rules manually but I am not able to fire workflow automatically.

How do I do this?

A: You can do this by using "Wait For" timer in workflow. You can select the time and days in advance to fire your workflow.

Question 172: Cannot load type in Callout

I make a callout dll using the CRM callout template in VS 2005 (http://blogs.msdn.com/arash/archive/2006/08/25/719626.asp x), this compile successfully, then I make the callout.config.xml and copy to the folder C:\Archivos de programa\Microsoft CRM\Server\bin\assembly and restart the iis and the WorkFlow Service of CRM, but when the callout executes log this error occurs in the Event Viewer:

Error: ISV code threw exception: assembly: CotizacionCallout.dll; class: CotizacionCallout.csCotizacionCallout; entity: opportunity, event: postcreate, exception: System.TypeLoadException: No se puede cargar el tipo CotizacionCallout.csCotizacionCallout del ensamblado CotizacionCallout, Version=1.0.0.0, Culture=neutral, PublicKeyToken=bfbf0db7a2c4ec23.

The assembly is strong named. I verify that with sn.exe -v and is compiled with the Framework 1.1, verified with ASMEX (An assembly explorer). I don't know what more can cause this problem, the class code is :

```
using System;
using System.Text;
using Microsoft.Crm.Callout;
using System.IO;
using System.Xml;
using System.Xml.Serialization;
using System.Web.Services.Protocols;

public class csCotizacionCallout : CrmCalloutBase
{

public override void PostCreate(CalloutUserContext
userContext,
CalloutEntityContext entityContext, string
postImageEntityXml)
{
TextWriter log =
TextWriter.Synchronized(File.AppendText(@"C:\Create.t
xt"));
log.WriteLine("PostCreate");
```

```
log.Close();
}

public override void PostUpdate(CalloutUserContext
userContext,
CalloutEntityContext entityContext, string
preImageEntityXml, string
postImageEntityXml)
{
TextWriter log =
TextWriter.Synchronized(File.AppendText(@"C:\Update.t
xt"));
log.WriteLine("PostUpdate");
log.WriteLine();
log.Close();
}
}
```

And the xml config file is:

```
<callout.config version="2.0">
<callout entity="opportunity" event="PostCreate">
<subscription assembly="CotizacionCallout.dll"
class="CotizacionCallout.csCotizacionCallout" >
</subscription>
</callout>
<callout entity="opportunity" event="PostUpdate">
<subscription assembly="CotizacionCallout.dll"
class="CotizacionCallout.csCotizacionCallout" >
</subscription>
</callout>
</callout.config>
```

How can I fix this?

A: You don't have a namespace definition in your code, so the type name of your callout is "csCotizacionCallout", while you have specified "CotizacionCallout.csCotizacionCallout" in the configuration file. You should either change the type name in the callout.config.xml to:

```
> <subscription assembly="CotizacionCallout.dll"
class="csCotizacionCallout" >
```

or add the namespace definition to your code:

```
namespace CotizacionCallout {
public class csCotizacionCallout : CrmCalloutBase {
....
}
```

}

Question 173: User Provided vs. System Calculated

When entering a new opportunity, the system calculated option is the default.

Is it possible to default to user provided instead?

A: Yes, it is very much possible. You may follow the following:
- Goto Settings --> Customization --> Customize Entities.
- Open Opportunity Entity.
- Goto Attributes , Open Attribute "Revenue".
- Here you can Change Default Value to User Provided.

Question 174: Creating own stored procedure in MSCRM database

I have a report that has been developed in SQL reporting services 2000 to be implemented for MS CRM 3.0. As there are lots of SQL statements with cursor and temp tables, I need to convert to a stored procedure.

Is it fine if I create a new stored procedure in MS CRM 3.0 database?

A: I suggest you avoid placing SPs direct in the CRM DB. You may create another DB called <yourorg>_REPORTS and place the SP in there. From your SRS report use:

```
exec <yourorg>_REPORTS..<spname>
```

Question 175: Condition expression problem

I try to retrieve data from crm using conditionexpression and it works but not the way I want. Unfortunately I would like it to retrieve all data that contains " passedparameter " but not equals.

For example: result will be string that contains " passedparameter "

sample result " passedparameter xxxx xxxxx " not only " passedparameter "

Here is my code below:

```
// Data from CRM with condition
ConditionExpression condition = new
ConditionExpression();
condition.AttributeName = "name";
condition.Operator = ConditionOperator.GreaterEqual;
condition.Values = new string[] { passedparameter };

FilterExpression crm_filter = new FilterExpression();
crm_filter.FilterOperator = LogicalOperator.Or;
crm_filter.Conditions = new ConditionExpression[] {
condition };

ColumnSet colsPK = new ColumnSet();
colsPK.Attributes = new string[] { "name",
"address1_postalcode", "address1_city",
"address1_country", "description",
"accountnumber", "revenue" };
QueryExpression queryPK = new QueryExpression();
queryPK.EntityName = EntityName.account.ToString();
queryPK.ColumnSet = colsPK;
queryPK.Criteria = crm_filter;

BusinessEntityCollection retrieved =
myService.RetrieveMultiple(queryPK);
```

How do I solve this?

A: You may do these two conditions:
```
ConditionExpression condition1 = new
ConditionExpression();
```

```
condition1.AttributeName = "name";
condition1.Operator = ConditionOperator.Like;
condition1.Values = new string[] { "%" +
passedparameter + "%" };

ConditionExpression condition2 = new
ConditionExpression();
condition2.AttributeName = "name";
condition2.Operator = ConditionOperator.NotEqual;
condition2.Values = new string[] { passedparameter };

FilterExpression crm_filter = new FilterExpression();
crm_filter.FilterOperator = LogicalOperator.And;
crm_filter.Conditions = new ConditionExpression[] {
condition1,
condition2 };
```

Question 176: Workflow assemblies

I'm trying to use the workflow on the CRM. I need to understand the Figure that represents an overview of workflow .NET Assemblies. Can you explain this Figure at the following URL: http://msdn.microsoft.com/library/?url=/library/en-us/CrmSdk3_0/htm/v3doworkflownetassemblies.asp, frame=true?

A: The figure describes the architecture of the CRM workflow engine. The developer (you) creates and modifies workflows using the Workflow Manager tool. You'll find it at the CRM server (go to programs/Microsoft CRM/Workflow Manager). When creating workflows you have two options:

1. Using built-in functionality to specify conditions and basic program flow.
2. Using custom .NET assemblies to perform more complex operations that cannot be handled with standard functions.

The arrow from Developer to Assemblies (named Generates) is the process of creating a piece of code (a custom workflow assembly) in .NET. The arrow from Developer to Workflow Config (named Modifies) means that you have to register your custom workflow assembly in this file to let the CRM Workflow Manager know about your custom assembly, its methods and how to call them, which is the arrow from Workflow Config to Assemblies (The config file "References" custom workflow assemblies).

The Workflow Manager "displays" (arrow from Workflow Config to Workflow Manager) the methods found in the workflow config file to use in a workflow. It means that you can write almost every function you need once and reference it in a workflow (the arrow from Workflow Rule to Assemblies). You create the whole workflow definition in the Workflow Manager (the definition is named "Workflow Rule" in the picture and the appropriate arrow is named "Creates").

Finally the Workflow Service (a Windows Service) reads all workflow rules and executes them if the workflow start conditions are met. It also loads your custom assembly and executes a method if you have specified to use it in the workflow rule. These are the two remaining arrows from Workflow Service to Workflow Rule and Assemblies.

Question 177: Problem with Conditions

I'm trying to create a query that takes two values from the same condition. If I do both values separately, it doesn't work. If I do this:

```
// Create the ConditionExpression.
ConditionExpression condition = new
ConditionExpression();
condition.AttributeName = "new_contactcategory";
condition.Operator = ConditionOperator.Equal;
condition.Values = new object[] { 4 };
```

it works.

If I do this:

```
// Create the ConditionExpression.
ConditionExpression condition = new
ConditionExpression();
condition.AttributeName = "new_contactcategory";
condition.Operator = ConditionOperator.Equal;
condition.Values = new object[] { 5 };
```

it works.

But, when I do this:

```
// Create the ConditionExpression.
ConditionExpression condition = new
ConditionExpression();
condition.AttributeName = "new_contactcategory";
condition.Operator = ConditionOperator.Equal;
condition.Values = new object[] { 4, 5 };
```

then it only pulls values for #4.

How can I make it so that it takes both?

A: Instead of using equal condition operator, try IN operator. Like:

```
condition.Operator = ConditionOperator.In;
```

Question 178: Report editing

What is the report editing tool in CRM?

Do we get it when installing vs.net, in vs2005, or do we get it as single tool?

A: To write/modify reports, Visual Studio .NET 2003 (or Visual Studio 2005) and Report Designer (a component of SQL Reporting Services) is the recommended development environment. These tools must be installed on the computer where the reports are authored. Visual Studio is the primary tool used to create or modify reports. You must also have access to Microsoft CRM to deploy the report.

Question 179: CMR 3.0 Database Diagram

Does a CMR 3.0 Database Diagram document exist?

A: Microsoft has released Microsoft Office Visio diagrams show the logical database structure for Microsoft CRM 3.0. The following diagrams are included:

A Crm3.0SFA.vsd, which shows the relationships for the core sales force automation entities: account, contact, lead, and opportunity.

A Crm3.0Activities.vsd, which shows the relationships for all activity entities: e-mail, letter, fax, phone call and task, as well as activity pointer, and queue.

A Crm3.0Org.vsd, which shows the relationships for the following organization entities: organization, business unit, user (system user), territory, team, and license.

A Crm3.0MA.vsd, which shows the relationships for the entities used in marketing automation: opportunity, lead, campaign, list, and activity pointer.

A Crm3.0Security.vsd, which shows the relationships for entities used for security: organization, license, role, privilege, and user (system user).

A Crm3.0SM.vsd, which shows the relationships for the entities used in service management: service, resource, calendar, equipment, appointment, service appointment, and site.

A Crm3.0QOI.vsd, which shows the relationships for quotes, orders and invoices: quote, order (sales order), opportunity, and invoice.

A Crm3.0CaseContract.vsd, which shows the relationships for case management: contract, case (incident), and subject.

A Crm3.0ProductCatalog.vsd, which shows the relationships for the product catalog: product, price level, subject, opportunity product, discount, sales literature, and product price level.

A Crm3.0Answers.vsd, which shows the relationships for the knowledge base: knowledge base article, subject, and sales literature.

You can download the diagrams from this location: http://www.microsoft.com/downloads/details.aspx? FamilyId=DA8D5048-615E-43C0-AB31-8FB5DA70216B&displaylang=en

Question 180: Import of quotes

I have a problem with the import of quotes out of our customers
ERP into CRM. A lot of fields seem to be required. A lot of them
I can get, but:

Do I have to generate unique Quote IDs and Revision IDs via the
Web Service?

The CRM-Forms do this automatically. The documentation says
the quote does not only require a (potential) customer but also a
contact of this customer. But I can't find the corresponding
attribute in the quote.

A: The quote and revision ID's are generated when saving the
quote, so you don't need to set them. It should be sufficient to
specify the quote name and the customer ID. Though a price list
(pricelevelid) is required in the CRM form, it's optional to set it
using the web services. There's no contact you need to set. It
should read that you can specify an account or a contact in the
customer field.

Question 181: C# Condition Expression

I've got a condition expression that works for me. It is:

```
// Set the condition for the retrieval to be when the
city in
the contact's address is Barrie.
condition.AttributeName = "address1_city";
condition.Operator = ConditionOperator.Like;
condition.Values = new string[] { "Cooper City" };
```

However, I am doing another project which requires something different. Basically, there is a Picklist field that we'd like to add in the condition. The picklist field is called "new_contactcategory". We only want to display records where that field is equal to "Alumni". It is a pick list, and the value of the text "Alumni" is 28.

How would that condition look in C#?

A: It should be almost the same as you're already using:

```
condition.AttributeName = "new_contactcategory";
condition.Operator = ConditionOperator.Equal;
condition.Values = new object[] { 28 };
```

Question 182: Getting the number of records in the collection

I'm writing a procedure that checks if there is another account with the same name of the one the user is inserting. I wrote the QueryExpression and it's working.

How can I get the number of the records found in my collection?

```
BusinessEntityCollection returnedAccounts =
service.RetrieveMultiple(query); returnedAccounts.
```

A: A BusinessEntityCollection contains an array of business entities, so the answer is:

```
int count = returnedAccounts.BusinessEntities.Length;
```

Question 183: Contact Conversion to a customer

I have just started working with CRM 3.0. I am looking to programmatically create a new contact and opportunity from an external web service call. There is no problem setting up a contact but the opportunity requires a customer object. Is there a way to convert my new contact object to a customer? It seems that the customer is an extension of a contact but ctype conversion is not accepted.

A: In MSCRM contacts map to Accounts, so you'll need to create a new account object, map the data fields you need, and then call the web service to create the new account, something like:

```
service = new CrmService();
service.Credentials =
System.Net.CredentialCache.DefaultCredentials;

account webAccount = new account();
webAccount.address1_city = "value";
webAccount.address1_name = "value";
etc.
Guid webAccountGuid = service.Create( webAccount );
```

A2: A customer object defines a relationship to either an account or a contact. The opportunities customerid property is a customer property, so you can assign both accounts and contacts. As you already have created a contact, your code will look like this:

```
opportunity.customerid = new Customer();
opportunity.customerid.type =
EntityName.contact.ToString();
opportunity.customerid.Value = contactid;
```

where contactid is the Guid you received when creating the contact. The important thing is that you must specifiy the type (EntityName.contact.ToString() or simply "contact"). Otherwise the CRM server does not know which entity is referenced. If you want to specify an account instead, set opportunity.customerid.type = EntityName.account.ToString();

Question 184: Filtered Views in ASP.NET 2.0 and IIS

I am having an issue with my filtered views displaying data. I am coding them on my PC, and they display the data correctly. But, when I put them on my Web Server (IIS) they don't display anything.

A: The filtered views rely on the SQL credentials being a valid CRM user. Make sure you are using proper credentials. I'm guessing your web site isn't setup for impersonation so you are "connecting" with the IIS service account.

Question 185: Retrieving multiple contacts

I've written (or am in the process of writing) an application that allows me to retrieve a list of contacts from CRM. Using examples I've been able to find, I was able to piece the application together to this point:

```
// Set the properties of the QueryExpression object.
query.EntityName = EntityName.contact.ToString();
query.ColumnSet = cols;
query.Criteria = filter;

// Retrieve the contacts.
BusinessEntityCollection contacts =
service.RetrieveMultiple(query);
```

Basically, I just want to be able to create a loop that will allow me to order through the list of contacts returned in the query and display them in a ShowMessage.

I know that "contacts" is the receiving entity for the record set.

What would the code look like that would allow me to "showmessage" the individual contacts from within the contacts entity?

A: You just need to do the following:

```
foreach(contact c in contacts.BusinessEntities) {
//process c
}
```

Question 186: Setting the linktype of DataSources at runtime

I have a button on a form. It's click-EventHandler contains a line:

```
CIRTRAStndTourOrderLine_ds.linkType(Transporteinheit.
valueStr() ? 3 /*
InnerJoin */ : 4 /* OuterJoin */);
```

Where "CIRTRAStndTourOrderLine_ds" is the data source generated by MorphX (CIRTRAStndTourOrderLine) is a table. "Transporteinheit" is a StringEdit.

The behavior I would like to achieve is, that if I enter something into the StringEdit it sets the linktype to InnerJoin otherwise to OuterJoin another table.

In MorphX I set the linktype to OuterJoin (as a default).

The problem is, that axapta simply does not change anything. I suppose I need some kind of refresh.

Is it possible?

A: If you are looking to refresh the datasource after you do the modification, yes. You would need to do something like this in your code:

```
CIRTRAStndTourOrderLine_ds.reSearch();
```

This should force a refresh (ie, re-run the query).

Question 187: "&" usage in isv.config

When I use an "&" in jscript that has been attached to a button added to the isv.config file the isv.config file errors.

How do I fix this?

A: The ampersand needs to be escaped with &

The easiest way to get to the correctly formatted code is to build a new XmlDocument, assign your code and save it to a file:

```
XmlDocument doc = new XmlDocument();

doc.AppendChild(doc.CreateXmlDeclaration("1.0", "UTF-8", null));

XmlElement root = doc.CreateElement("root");

doc.AppendChild(root);

XmlElement ampersand =
doc.CreateElement("ampersand");

ampersand.InnerText = "&";

root.AppendChild(ampersand);

doc.Save("c:\\ampersand.xml");
```

Open it with a standard editor (Notepad is fine, not IE, it will recognize the encoding) and copy the encoded string.

Question 188: Canceling contract

I am currently rewriting a vb.net service that updates crm data so that we can implement crm 3.0. When I attempt to cancel a contract, I get the following error:

"Server was unable to process request. 0x80043203 The state of the contract is invalid".

Here is my code:

```
Private Sub CancelContract(ByVal ContractID As
String)
Dim Contract As New CrmSdk.contract
Dim CancelDate As String = DateTime.Now.ToString("s")
CancelDate = CancelDate.Substring(0, 10)

Try

ContractID = FormatGUID(ContractID)
Contract.contractid = New crmSDK.Key()
Contract.contractid.Value = New Guid(ContractID)
Contract.cancelon = New crmSDK.CrmDateTime()
Contract.cancelon.Value = CancelDate & "T00:00:00"
Contract.statecode = New crmSDK.ContractStateInfo()
Contract.statecode.Value =
crmSDK.ContractState.Canceled
crmSvc.Update(Contract)

Catch err As
System.Web.Services.Protocols.SoapException
SendMailForError("Sub CancelContract: " & vbCrLf &
"CancelContract Xml: " & "SoapException: " &
err.Message & " " &
err.Detail.OuterXml & " Source: " & err.Source)

Catch err As Exception
SendMailForError("Sub CancelContract: " & vbCrLf &
"CancelContract Xml: " & err.ToString())
End Try
End Sub
```

How can I fix this?

A: You need to use the SetStateContractRequest class in a service.Execute statement to change the state. This is the same for all entities (SetStateAccountRequest, SetStateContactRequest and so on).

Question 189: ISV and JavaScript

String from ISV.config:

```
<Button Title="Test" Icon="/_imgs/ico_18_debug.gif"
JavaScript="alert('test')" />
```

This works fine. Importing into CRM system without trouble.

But this one:

```
<Button Title="Test" Icon="/_imgs/ico_18_debug.gif"
JavaScript="var wdApp =
new ActiveXObject("Word.Application");" />
```

Don't work. During importing I get error: "Check that file format is valid".

Why?

A: You use around Word.Application, consider using:

```
<Button Title="Test" Icon="/_imgs/ico_18_debug.gif"
JavaScript="var wdApp
= new ActiveXObject('Word.Application');" />
```

Question 190: Online or Offline

I've got a demo system setup and have made a few changes to showcase CRM. One of the things I have done is tied the Contact form into a simple website that locates the contact's website login and displays it. This works fine. What I want to be able to do is hide this IFrame when the CRM Client is in Offline mode since a connection to the website is no longer guaranteed.

Is there a way to programmatically check on form load if the CRM Client is operating in online or offline mode?

A: Yes, the method is named IsOnline. The SDK documentation contains it in the topic "Global Methods".

Question 191: Using NOT operator with Advanced Find

We can group ROW in Advanced Find with AND or OR operator.

How can I use NOT operator?

For example: I need to find LEADs which have activity LETTER with some conditions AND NOT have activity PHONE CALL with some conditions.

A: This is a shortcoming of the current advanced find. There isn't a NOT operator, so the query you're trying to build is not possible. The best you can do is creating a report for it.

Index

www.ingramcontent.com/pod-product-compliance
Lightning Source LLC
Chambersburg PA
CBHW051050050326
40690CB00006B/666